Why Does God Want My Money

Why Does God Want My Money

How God Transforms Our Hearts Through Generosity

Charles D. Harris

Kingdom Manna Press

Scripture Versions

In some instances, the author has added emphasis to Scripture quotations for clarity. These are noted as "emphasis added."

ISBN 979-8-9946808-0-3 (Paperback)

ISBN 979-8-9946808-2-7 (Hardcover)

ISBN 979-8-9946808-4-1 (eBook)

Disclaimer

This book is designed to provide inspiration, encouragement, and biblical teaching regarding personal finances and generosity. It is sold with the understanding that neither the author nor the publisher is engaged in rendering professional financial, legal, tax, or accounting advice.

The financial principles and personal stories in this book are provided for general informational and inspirational purposes only. Every financial situation is unique, and readers should consult qualified professionals regarding their specific circumstances before making financial decisions.

The testimonies and stories in this book reflect real experiences. Individual results will vary. Past outcomes described are not guarantees of future results. The spiritual and financial principles taught are based on the author's interpretation of Scripture and personal experience. Readers are encouraged to study the Bible for themselves and seek guidance from their local church leadership regarding application of these principles.

While the author has made every effort to provide accurate biblical interpretation and practical guidance at the time of publication, neither the author nor the publisher assumes any

Endorsement by Craig Hill

I have known Charles Harris as a good friend and faithful minister at Family Foundations International for over 15 years. In his book, *Why Does God Want My Money?* Charles does a masterful job of uncovering hidden truths from the Bible that answer some of the most pressing questions many people ask regarding money. In this book, you will learn not only practical answers to your financial questions but also God's heart behind those answers. In this book, you will learn:

- To understand God's perspective on money
- How to navigate the most common financial struggles many people face
- How to embrace generosity and a focus on blessing others even when it seems difficult
- How to be a faithful steward of the resources God has placed in your hands

I highly recommend this book to anyone who would like to discover God's heart of generosity and learn how to manage money from a Kingdom of God perspective. This book will give you the knowledge and tools to properly steward the resources God has given you so that, in the end, you might hear the Lord's words spoken to you, "*Well done, good and faithful servant!*"

Craig Hill
Author and International Conference Speaker
Founder of Family Foundations International
https://craighill.org/

Endorsement from Donna Zorn

It is a great pleasure to write for my friend, Charles Harris. I have known Charles since 2003. We worshiped together under the leadership of Pastor David Mitts in our congregation, One New Man. During these years we all have grown much in our faith, understanding the Word, and encouraging to each other.

Charles is one of the most faithful men I know. He is a natural teacher about offerings. His teachings are Holy Spirit led from the Old and New Testament. I can't count the number of times I have said to him, "You need to write a book."

When I became the Executive Director of Covenant Keepers, a marriage restoration ministry, I realized how much Charles' teachings meant to me. Let me tell you a personal testimony. On New Year's Eve, I attended a street festival in my area of town. Before I left home, I gave a $200 year end offering to Covenant Keepers. I then put my credit card in my pocket along with a $100 bill. I made a couple of small purchases. Once I returned home, I emptied my pockets. Much to my surprise, there was NO $100 bill. My immediate thought was, 'I hope the person who found it needed it more than I did.' I began to realize IF I had lost the $100 bill first I would never have made that year end offering. Once again, it is because of God using Charles' teachings and my growth that I am able to praise the Lord. I am no longer following the pattern of this world but I am being transformed by the renewing of my mind -Ro 12:2. This book will be a great tool in your transformation process.

Pastor Donna Zorn

Executive Director

CKministry.org

Contents

Part III
Nations
Hearing God Direct You to Bless Others

Author's Note

A Word About the Stories in This Book

Throughout this book, you'll encounter stories that illustrate biblical principles about money and generosity. I want to be transparent about how these stories work.

Biblical Stories

Every biblical account in this book is historically accurate and properly cited. The widow who came to Elisha, the boy with five loaves and two fish, Ruth and Boaz, Jacob's twenty years with Laban—these are not illustrations or parables. They are Scripture, and they happened exactly as God's Word records them.

Modern Stories

The contemporary stories—people like Regina facing impossible bills, Carlos a warehouse supervisor with money controlling his thoughts, Candace wrestling with sleepless anxiety, Nicole discovering overflow—are illustrative narratives crafted to help you see how biblical principles work in modern contexts.

Like Jesus, who taught through parables about farmers, merchants, and families, I've used narrative to make God's voice about money clearer and more accessible. These aren't documentary accounts or testimonials claiming, "this specific event happened to this specific person on this specific date." The stories re illustrations designed to bring biblical truth to life.

Why This Approach?

Jesus rarely taught financial principles through abstract theology. He told stories: a shrewd manager, a generous Samaritan, a faithful steward, a foolish rich man. These parables weren't lying—they were truth wrapped in narrative that lodges in the heart deeper than mere facts ever could.

Some of the modern stories in this book are inspired by real situations I've witnessed or heard about through years of ministry. Others are composites representing common patterns many Christians experience. Still others are created specifically to illustrate a biblical principle in contemporary terms.

But every story—whether biblical history or modern parable—points to the same truth: God's voice about finances is trustworthy, and His principles work when applied with faith and obedience.

What About My Personal Story?

My own 3 AM crisis that you read about in the Preface? That's real. My spouse's and my involvement in orphan care and supporting trafficking victims? That's our actual life and ministry.

But this book isn't primarily my memoir. It's about helping you hear God's voice about money and respond in obedience. Where I've shared personal experience, it's to establish credibility and connection. The focus remains on biblical truth, not my biography.

The Truth That Matters

Whether a story comes from Scripture, from personal experience, or from my imagination crafting a parable to illustrate truth, what matters is this: Does it accurately represent God's character? Does it faithfully reflect biblical principles? Does it help you hear His voice more clearly?

The widow with oil didn't need her story to be recent to teach the truth about provision. The boy with loaves didn't need to be your contemporary to demonstrate the power of small offerings given in faith. And Regina's impossible math doesn't need to be documentable to help you see that God cares about YOUR bills.

My Prayer

I pray that these stories—biblical and modern, historical and illustrative—will help you recognize God's faithfulness in your own financial journey and give you courage to trust His voice with your resources.

The principles are real. The God behind them is real. The transformation He offers is real.

And that's what matters most.

Foreword by David Mitts

In the realm of the Spirit, vision determines reality. How we see things or better perceive them defines what they are to us and also in us. Pastor Charles is a man of vision. His unique perspectives on the financial realm of life and its impact on our walk with God are truly transformational. The Apostle Paul tells us to be transformed by the renewal of our mind (Romans 12:1-2). The fresh perspective Charles shares with us in this book will, if we allow it, to bring us a freedom in our relationship with God.

My wife Lisa and I have had the privilege of serving in ministry with Pastor Charles since 2003. He and his wife, Perry, have always been stars in our heavenly realm. I have seen them being abased and abounding, and they truly know how to be content and trusting wholly in God's provision for life's inevitable situations and challenges.

In these days, that we know are close to the return of Jesus to this world, there are certainly going to be many challenges to the area of provision. This is an hour to truly invest in our understanding of how God relates to our money. We know that the Antichrist will attack in this area, and we need to be prepared in both spirit and truth.

Get ready to dive deeply into truth and be transformed in your spirit as Charles gently and lovingly reveals the words of God regarding our hearts and how to keep them pure in the hour ahead!

Pastor David Mitts
One New Man Ministries
Founder of Destiny House Restoration Center

Preface

I lay awake at 3 AM, staring at the ceiling while my wife slept peacefully beside me. The question wouldn't leave me alone: "If God owns everything, why does He keep asking for mine?"

The offering plate at church felt like a demand I couldn't afford to meet. Every sermon about tithing triggered a familiar knot in my stomach. Bills were due. My paycheck was stretched. And God wanted His 10%?

For years, I wrestled with guilt, confusion, and secret resentment. I loved God. I believed in His Word. But His instructions about money felt like one more burden on an already strained budget.

Then I discovered something that changed everything.

This book is about that discovery. If you've ever felt the same tension—loving God but struggling with what He asks regarding your finances—this book is for you.

The answer isn't what I expected. And it has nothing to do with God needing your money

Charles D. Harris

Acknowledgments

First and foremost, I want to express my gratitude to God for inspiring me to emphasize His heart on giving and generosity. I thank Jesus (Yeshua) for allowing us to express our generosity with joy through the freedom He has provided. I appreciate the Holy Spirit for teaching, training, and guidance on the truths of Scripture related to generosity.

This book is dedicated to my beloved wife, Perry, who has been a constant source of inspiration and support through life's ups and downs. She is an incredible wife, mother, grandmother, and friend to many. Her loving encouragement was essential in helping me complete this mission. Perry, I love you dearly.

I would also like to acknowledge my children—Robert, Dominique, Shiloh, Talia, and Charles Jr.—and my grandchildren—Amiyah, Harmony, Dailey, Emberly and Loveah —who motivated me throughout the writing process and helped me reach this milestone. Thank you all.

Additionally, I want to honor my parents, Abraham and Hattie Harris, who have faithfully guided their children's spiritual paths through thick and thin, trusting in the Lord's provision.

Furthermore, I extend my appreciation to our faith community at One New Man Ministries, especially my pastors, David and

Lisa Mitts, and Donna Zorn's faithful prayer support. I am grateful for the faith-filled support of all our dear friends within our community who have listened to my messages on generosity and giving, inspiring me to compile them into this book. Thank you.

Introduction

Learning to Hear God's Voice About Money

Rachel stared at her laptop screen, the cursor blinking in her online banking portal. Rent was due in three days. Her checking account balance: $1,847. The rent: $1,650. That left $197 for groceries, gas, and everything else until her next paycheck in two weeks.

The tithe would be $184.70.

She'd done this calculation a hundred times in the past month, always arriving at the same impossible math. If she tithed, she'd have $12.30 left. Twelve dollars and thirty cents to feed herself and keep gas in her car for two weeks.

Her finger hovered over the "Transfer Funds" button.

This is crazy, a voice whispered in her mind. *God doesn't expect you to starve. Be reasonable. Just this once, skip it.*

But another voice, quieter but somehow clearer, had been speaking to her all month. During her morning quiet time, she'd read Jesus' words: "Your heavenly Father knows that you need all these things." The verse had captured her attention, refusing to let go. Last Sunday, her pastor's sermon about trusting God seemed aimed directly at her situation. Yesterday, her small group leader had shared how God provided for her family during a tight season—right after she'd asked Rachel how things were going financially.

Rachel closed her eyes. "God, are You really asking me to do this? With $12 left?"

The peace that settled over her didn't match her circumstances. It didn't make the math work. But somehow, at that moment, she knew which voice she was hearing.

She clicked "Transfer Funds."

Rachel's decision that night wasn't about following a rule. It was about recognizing God's voice and choosing to respond. She'd heard Him speaking through Scripture, through teaching, through counsel, and through supernatural peace that defied her panic.

This book is about that choice—learning to hear God's voice about your finances and responding with obedient action.

Not religious obligations. Not transactional formulas. Not guilt-driven compliance. But genuine relationship that transforms how you relate to money and to God.

The Foundation: A Heart Willing to Give

When God invited His people to build a place where He would dwell among them, He didn't demand contributions. He didn't mandate percentages. He didn't threaten potential consequences.

He issued an invitation:

> "Tell the Israelites to bring me an offering. You are to receive the offering for me from everyone whose heart prompts them to give." (Ex. 25:2).

Everyone whose heart prompts them to give.

When the work began, Moses announced:

> "Everyone who is willing is to bring the LORD an offering..." (Ex. 35:5)

. The text repeats the phrase:

> "All who were willing...everyone who was willing..." (Ex. 35:21-29).

God wanted willing hearts, not reluctant compliance.

Centuries later, Paul wrote about this same principle:

> "Each of you should give what you have decided in your heart to give, not reluctantly or under compulsion, for God loves a cheerful giver" (2 Cor. 9:7).

Not reluctantly. Not under compulsion. But cheerfully—from a heart that trusts God's promises more than circumstances.

Here's why this matters: You cannot hear God's voice clearly about finances if your heart is unwilling to obey what He says.

An unwilling heart allows circumstances to dominate. Fear drowns out God's voice before He finishes speaking. Every financial decision becomes a survival calculation rather than an opportunity to hear and obey.

But a willing heart creates space to actually hear. Not blind obedience that ignores wisdom. Not reckless compliance that abandons discernment. But genuine willingness that says, "God, if this is really You speaking, I want to obey. Even if it doesn't make sense. Even if my math doesn't work. Even if I'm afraid."

That willingness is what allows you to distinguish God's voice from every competing authority clamoring for control of your wallet.

A willing heart transforms financial obedience from religious duty into intimate worship. It changes the question from "How much do I have to give?" to "How much do You want me to give?" From distant compliance to close partnership.

That shift—from reluctant obligation to willing devotion—is what this book is designed to create.

The Three-Dimensional Journey

When Jesus was asked about the greatest commandment, He quoted the Shema:

> "Hear, O Israel: The Lord our God, the Lord is one. Love the Lord your God with all your heart and with all your soul and with all your mind and with all your strength." Then He added: "Love your neighbor as yourself. There is no commandment greater than these." (Mark 12:29-31)

Notice the progression: Love God with everything → Love yourself rightly → Love your neighbor from that overflow.

Finances follow this exact pattern.

Part I: Heaven teaches you to hear God's voice calling you to worship Him with your finances. This is where heart willingness begins—where you learn to respond with genuine devotion rather than fearful obligation. Until you learn to love God with your finances, the rest of this journey won't make sense.

Part II: House teaches you to hear God's promises about provision for your household. Jesus said to love your neighbor *as yourself*—which assumes you love yourself rightly. Many Christians can worship God with firstfruits but panic about their own provision. This part shows you how to trust God's promises about your bills even when your math doesn't work.

Part III: Nations teaches you to hear God directing you toward others. Once you've learned to worship Him and trust His provision for your household, He begins directing you to bless people and communities from the overflow He's created. This isn't an obligation-based charity—it's hearing His voice say, "Bless them with what I gave you," and responding from a place of willing devotion.

Heaven → House → Nations. The progression Jesus established, applied specifically to finances.

What Happened to Rachel

Rachel didn't know this progression when she clicked

"Transfer Funds" with $12.30 left to her name. She just knew she'd heard God's voice and chosen to respond.

The next morning, a friend texted offering to buy Rachel groceries. Three days later, a former client called with unexpected freelance work. By the end of two weeks, Rachel had more in her account than when she started.

But here's what matters more: Rachel's heart had shifted. God's promises—"Your heavenly Father knows that you need all these things"—remained rooted despite the storm of circumstances around them. She'd stopped calculating what she had to give and started listening for what God was inviting her to give.

That's what this book is designed to create—not behavior modification, but heart transformation. Not religious obligation, but genuine relationship. Not fearful compliance, but willing devotion.

The Invitation

Remember what God told Moses: "Everyone whose heart prompts them to give."

That's the spirit of this entire book. Not obligation, not manipulation, not guilt, but rather, an invitation to allow God's promises to become stronger than your circumstances. For His voice to become clearer than your fear, and your giving to flow from cheerful willingness rather than reluctant compliance.

God is inviting you into a different way of relating to money. A journey where your finances become one of the primary ways you hear His voice and respond in faith. A progression that will teach you to love Him with your wallet, trust His provision for your household, and bless your neighbor from overflow.

He's inviting you. And He's looking for hearts that are willing to respond. Is yours?

Part I

Heaven

Hearing God Call You to Worship

Every financial decision you make is ultimately a choice about which voice you'll obey.

Not which advice seems smartest. Not which option feels safest. But which voice you trust most deeply.

Fear's voice screams loudest during sleepless nights about bills and empty accounts. Culture's voice whispers constantly through advertising and social media that you deserve more, need more, should have more. Comparison's voice makes you feel perpetually behind.

But God's voice speaks differently. Quieter than the others. Steadier. Calling you to something the competing voices can never offer, worship.

Not the worship of singing songs on Sunday mornings. The worship of surrendering your finances as an act of devotion.

The worship of loving Him with your whole heart—including your bank account.

Learning Which Voice to Follow

Part I establishes the foundation everything else builds on: learning to recognize God's voice about finances and choosing to obey what you hear.

You'll discover your identity as God's royal child. You'll learn what it means to choose between serving God or money. You'll understand the rhythm He designed for blessing. And you'll begin distinguishing His voice from every competing authority clamoring for control of your wallet.

This is heart work. Until you know which voice controls your finances, you can't move forward into trusting His provision for your household or blessing others from overflow.

The Question That Changes Everything

Which voice are you following with your money?

The answer reveals which voice you trust with your life.

Chapter 1
The King's Wallet

Candace lay awake at 2 AM, running numbers in her head for the third time that night. As a dental hygienist supporting two teenagers alone, every dollar mattered. The mortgage payment loomed in five days. Her son's basketball shoes had worn through completely. The car registration was overdue.

Then her pastor's sermon about tithing echoed in her memory: "Honor God with the firstfruits of your income."

Candace's stomach clenched. "Give God 10% when I can't manage 100% of my bills? That seems impossible."

She had no idea that, three months later, she would experience a transformation that would shock her—not because her circumstances dramatically improved, but because she discovered her true identity. She wasn't a desperate beggar scrambling for scraps. She was royalty in God's kingdom, designed to be a generous giver.

Why God Rules Like No Other King

> "For the Lord is a great God, and a great King above all gods" (Ps. 95:3, ESV).

God's kingdom operates on revolutionary principles that completely transform your relationship with money. Faith, hope, and love power His kingdom—not political connections, social status, or bank account balances.

Your royal identity means managing resources for the richest King in the universe. Your value as His citizen isn't determined by your net worth or career achievements, but by your faithful stewardship of whatever He entrusts to you.

Your Generous Design

> "So God created man in his own image, in the image of God he created him; male and female he created them" (Gen. 1:27, ESV).

Since God is fundamentally a giver, you are designed to be a giver. This isn't a religious obligation—it's spiritual DNA embedded in your very nature.

> "For God so loved the world, that he gave his only Son, that whoever believes in him should not perish but have eternal life" (John 3:16, ESV).

God's ultimate expression of generosity flowed from perfect love, not religious duty. When you live according to this divine design, you find freedom and joy in what you give, not just what you receive.

Royal Identity Flows from Proper Reverence

Your generous DNA isn't just about design—it's rooted in something deeper: the fear of the Lord.

> "In the fear of the LORD one has strong confidence, and his children will have a refuge" (Prov. 14:26, ESV).

Notice that connection? When you learn proper reverence for God, confidence follows. Not arrogance—confidence. The kind that allows you to give generously because you trust your Father's provision. The kind that transforms beggar mentality into royal identity.

The world's system operates on fear of scarcity: "What if I don't have enough?" God's kingdom operates on fear of the Lord: "My Father owns everything, and He delights in providing for His children." That's not wishful thinking—that's royal identity rooted in proper reverence.

Tom spent thirty-eight years enslaved to fear of scarcity, because his father taught him to fear running out. When Tom learned proper fear of the Lord—reverence for God's character and promises—his identity shifted from beggar to royalty.

This is what Solomon meant when he wrote:

> "The reward for humility and fear of the LORD is riches and honor and life" (Prov. 22:4, ESV).

The riches aren't always financial. Often, they're the wealth of royal identity—knowing who you are as God's child, living with confidence that comes from proper reverence, experiencing the life that flows from trusting your Father.

When You Put Away Foreign Gods, God Becomes Your Defense

Jacob faced a crisis. He'd just witnessed violence in Shechem that endangered his entire household. Enemies surrounded them. Retaliation seemed inevitable. His family was vulnerable, exposed, and outnumbered.

God's instruction was specific:

> "Arise, go up to Bethel and dwell there. Make an altar there to the God who appeared to you when you fled from your brother Esau" (Gen. 35:1 ESV).

But before Jacob could obey, something had to change in his household. His family was carrying foreign gods—idols that represented competing allegiances, divided loyalties, alternative sources of security.

Jacob understood what God was asking: You cannot serve Me and also hedge your bets with other gods. You cannot live in proper fear of the LORD while clinging to fear-based alternatives.

His command to his household was direct:

> "Put away the foreign gods that are among you and purify yourselves and change your garments. Then let us arise and go up to

> Bethel, so that I may make there an altar to the God who answers me in the day of my distress and has been with me wherever I have gone" (Gen. 35:2-3 ESV).

They responded completely:

> "So they gave to Jacob all the foreign gods that they had, and the rings that were in their ears. Jacob hid them under the terebinth tree that was near Shechem" (Gen. 35:4 ESV).

Then something remarkable happened as they journeyed to Bethel:

> "And as they journeyed, a terror from God fell upon the cities that were around them, so that they did not pursue the sons of Jacob" (Gen. 35:5 ESV).

When Jacob's household put away their foreign gods and committed themselves completely to the one true God, the LORD Himself became their defense. The enemies who should have pursued them were struck with supernatural terror. God's fear fell on those who threatened His people.

The same principle applies to your finances today. Fear of scarcity is a foreign god—an alternative source of security that competes with trust in God's provision. When you put away that foreign god and embrace proper fear of the LORD, something shifts. The "enemies" that pursue you—anxiety about bills, panic about provision, midnight calculations—lose their power. God's peace replaces their terror.

Royal identity isn't just about knowing who you are. It's about putting away every competing allegiance that undermines your confidence in your Father's provision. When you serve God alone, He becomes your defense against every threatening circumstance.

Choosing Your Master Means Choosing Your Fear

Here's the question you must ask yourself: Which fear will control you?

Scripture presents two options: fear of the Lord or fear of death. You're going to live in a reverent awe of something. The question is, what?

> "Since therefore the children share in flesh and blood, he himself likewise partook of the same things, that through death he might destroy the one who has the power of death, that is, the devil, and deliver all those who through fear of death were subject to lifelong slavery" (Heb. 2:14-15, ESV).

Fear of death creates lifelong slavery. Not physical death necessarily—but the fear that you'll run out, that you won't have enough, that disaster will leave you destitute if you don't hoard and control everything yourself.

> "Better is a little with the fear of the LORD than

> great treasure and trouble with it" (Prov. 15:16, ESV).

You can have treasure (decent income) but live with constant trouble (anxiety, broken relationships, midnight panic). When you choose proper fear of the Lord—reverence, trust, worship—the trouble lifts even before your financial circumstances dramatically change.

Every time you choose which master to serve, you're choosing which fear controls you. Choose reverence for God. It's the only fear that leads to freedom.

Tom's Thirty-Eight Years of Fear

Tom had worked at the same factory for sixteen years, maintaining machines that stamped automotive parts. Steady work. Decent pay. Nothing remarkable.

But Tom carried a weight that had nothing to do with his job and everything to do with his father's voice in his head.

"Hold on to your money tight, son. You never know what disasters are coming."

His father survived the Great Depression as a child. That experience had shaped every financial decision he'd made—and every piece of advice he'd drilled into Tom since childhood. Save everything. Trust no one. Give nothing away. The world is dangerous, and your bank account is your only defense.

For thirty-eight years, Tom had lived by those rules.

He and his wife Janet had $47,000 in savings—a number that should have brought peace but instead created constant anxiety. Was it enough? What if the factory closed? What if the car died? What if, what if, what if?

Tom tithed occasionally—maybe three or four times a year when guilt overwhelmed him during particularly convicting sermons. But it always felt like ripping off a bandage. Every dollar he placed in the offering plate was a dollar that couldn't protect him from his father's imagined disasters.

Janet had stopped mentioning their church's mission fund campaign. Their marriage had become as tight as Tom's grip on their finances. Their kids had learned not to ask Dad for anything extra.

Tom was surviving, but he wasn't living. And he knew it.

The Sermon That Wouldn't Let Go

The visiting missionary's sermon wasn't particularly eloquent. But one phrase lodged itself in Tom's mind like a splinter: "You can't out-give God, but you can out-fear Him."

Tom sat in the pew feeling exposed. How did this stranger know?

The missionary continued: "Some of you are holding onto money so tightly because you're fearful of the future. You think your savings account is your security. But every time you choose fear over faith, you're declaring that God isn't trustworthy."

Tom's chest tightened. He glanced at Janet. She was crying quietly.

That night, Tom couldn't sleep. He went downstairs and opened his Bible—something he rarely did outside of church. He wasn't sure what he was looking for, but his eyes landed on a verse someone had underlined years ago:

> "Each of you should give what you have decided in your heart to give, not reluctantly or under compulsion, for God loves a cheerful giver" (2 Cor. 9:7).

Grudgingly. That was exactly how he gave—when he gave at all.

Tom sat on his couch until after 2 AM, calculator in hand, running different scenarios. What if he tithed his full paycheck? His monthly income was $3,800. Ten percent would be $380.

His father's voice rose immediately: *That's foolishness. That's four car payments. That's a month of groceries. That's a disaster waiting to happen.*

But another voice—quieter, steadier—whispered something different: *That's worship. That's trust. That's freedom.*

Tom made a decision that night that terrified him. Starting with his next paycheck, he would tithe the full 10%—not occasionally, not grudgingly, but first and cheerfully. Before the mortgage. Before savings. Before everything.

He would either discover that God was trustworthy, or he would prove his father right.

The Six-Month Transformation

Month One: Tom wrote the tithe check on Friday morning before work, hands shaking. He placed it in the offering plate Sunday, feeling simultaneously liberated and nauseated. Walking to their car after service, Janet squeezed his hand. "How do you feel?"

"Fearful," Tom admitted. "But... also free? Like I finally stopped trying to be God and let God be God."

They made it throughout the month. Barely. But they made it.

Month Two: Tom's truck needed new brakes—$450. Tom stared at the quote, his father's voice roaring: *See? This is what happens when you give away the money you need.*

But Tom's brother-in-law did the work for $240—$210 saved. More than half his tithe. Tom hung up the phone, hands trembling. Coincidence? Maybe. But Tom felt something shift inside him.

Month Three: Janet approached him carefully one evening. "Tom, I've been watching you these past few months. You seem... different."

Tom realized she was right. He'd stopped calculating worst-case scenarios constantly. He'd stopped checking their savings account balance three times a day. The knot in his stomach that had been his constant companion for thirty-eight years had loosened.

Not because they had more money. They actually had slightly less. But because he'd discovered something his father had never taught him: Security doesn't come from what you control. It comes from trusting the One who controls everything.

Over the next three months, provision came through unexpected channels: Tom's supervisor offered him a promotion to lead the third-shift maintenance team—$4,200 monthly salary, a $400 increase that almost exactly matched his tithe. A coworker starting a side business doing small engine repairs asked Tom to help on weekends—splitting profits 50-50, bringing in about $600 monthly.

Month Six: The transformation wasn't just financial. Tom's relationship with Janet had changed. They talked about money without fighting. They made decisions without fear dominating every conversation. His kids noticed, too. When his daughter mentioned needing money for a school trip, Tom said yes without the usual lecture about responsibility and sacrifice. She looked shocked.

Most remarkably, Tom found himself looking for ways to help others. When his elderly neighbor mentioned she couldn't afford to fix her garage door, Tom offered to do it for free on a Saturday. When his church announced a special missions offering, Tom gave $500 without anxiety.

His father had taught him that holding tightly to his finances brought security. Tom discovered the opposite was true: Giving freely brought freedom.

Royal Identity vs. Beggar Mentality

The difference between Tom's before and after wasn't just behavior—it was identity.

Beggar Mentality says:

- I must scrape and scramble for every dollar
- Resources are scarce and I must hoard what I have
- Giving means I'll have less
- My security comes from what I've accumulated
- I'm one disaster away from ruin
- Life is about survival and accumulation

Royal Identity declares:

- I'm a child of the King who owns everything
- I'm managing resources that ultimately belong to Him
- Giving is privilege and worship, not sacrifice
- My security comes from my Father's character
- I'm positioned to bless others because I'm blessed
- Life is about stewardship and significance

Tom had spent thirty-eight years living as a beggar, even though he'd been royalty all along. The transformation happens when you finally believe what God says about your identity—and start living accordingly.

How to Access God's Economic System

The world's economy operates on fear, scarcity, and competition. God's economy functions through giving and receiving, trusting in His faithful provision.

> "Give, and it will be given to you. A good measure, pressed down, shaken together and running over, will be poured into your lap. For with the measure you use, it will be measured to you" (Luke 6:38).

When you release seeds of faith through generous giving, you position yourself for God's provision in forms that include financial increase, community support, spiritual peace, and character growth.

Your Royal Heart

> "For where your treasure is, there your heart will be also" (Matt. 6:21).

God doesn't need your money—He wants your heart aligned with His generous character. When you give willingly and joyfully, you position yourself to experience His provision in ways that extend far beyond material wealth.

Giving demonstrates your heart's trust in God's provision and character. Your generous actions become worship, expressions of faith, and love in practical form.

Candace's Royal Discovery

Candace decided to trust her royal identity rather than her circumstances. She began tithing faithfully despite tight finances.

The first month was terrifying. She wrote the tithe check on the same day her mortgage was due, whispering a prayer as she sealed the envelope: "God, I'm trusting You with this."

Nothing dramatic happened immediately. Bills still came. Her son still needed shoes. The car registration was still waiting.

But Candace noticed something strange: She wasn't panicking. The 2 AM anxiety sessions stopped. She'd decided to follow God's voice instead of fear's whisper, and somehow that decision brought peace even before provision appeared.

By the end of the second month, small things started shifting. Her dentist's boss mentioned they had more patients than usual—would she be willing to work an extra day weekly? That brought an additional $520 monthly. Her ex-husband, who'd been sporadic with child support, suddenly started paying consistently. Her landlord approached about helping manage his rental properties in exchange for $200 monthly rent reduction.

Three months after she started tithing, Candace calculated the math one evening. Her effective income had increased by $720 monthly—significantly more than the $320 she was giving away in tithes.

But the real transformation wasn't the numbers. Candace had stopped seeing herself as a struggling single mother begging for help. She recognized her true identity as a royal daughter managing resources for the richest King in the universe.

Her teenagers noticed the change. Her fifteen-year-old son asked one evening, "Mom, why aren't you worried about money anymore?"

Candace thought about how to answer. "I stopped trusting my bank account and started trusting God. Turns out, He's better at math than I am."

But it was deeper than that. Candace had discovered that royal identity changes everything about how you handle money. Beggars hoard from fear. Royalty gives out of confidence. Beggars panic when resources run low. Royalty trusts the King's provision.

Six months into her journey, Candace faced an unexpected test. Her car needed $800 for repairs—money she didn't have. Her old self would have panicked, borrowed, or stopped tithing to cover it.

Instead, Candace prayed: "God, I'm Your daughter. You know I need this repair. I'm going to keep tithing and trust You to work it out."

Two days later, her brother called. He'd just received a bonus at work and felt prompted to help her. Could he send $800?

Candace hung up the phone and cried—not from relief, but from recognition. She wasn't a beggar God had reluctantly helped. She was royalty whose Father delighted in providing for her.

Your Call to Royal Living

God has designed you as a giver, created to reflect His generous nature in practical ways. When you operate according to His kingdom's principles rather than the world's fear-based system, you break free from anxiety and step into joy.

Generous living transcends financial exchange—it becomes worship, trust, and love demonstrated through action. When you live according to your divine design, giving joyfully and faithfully, you witness God's provision in ways that often exceed expectations.

Your generous design doesn't exempt you from life's realities —it provides perspective, community, and spiritual resources for navigating them with grace and peace.

The choices before you are clear: Will you continue operating in the world's fear-based system of accumulation and anxiety? Or will you step into your royal identity as a generous child of the King who owns everything?

Tom discovered that freedom comes through releasing, not grasping. Candace experienced that royal identity transforms panic into peace.

Your royal identity awaits your decision to live accordingly.

Questions for Your Heart

1. Which system has been controlling your financial decisions—the world's or God's?
2. How would your life change if you truly believed you were designed to be a giver?
3. Where do you see "beggar mentality" in your approach to finances—and what would "royal identity" look like instead?
4. What's one way you could practice generous living this week?

Prayer for Royal Givers

Heavenly Father, thank You for welcoming me into Your kingdom as Your child and designing me in Your generous image. Help me serve You with everything I am—my time, talents, and resources.

Teach me to seek Your kingdom first in every decision. Help me trust in Your faithful provision and free me from financial fears that keep me from generous living. Fill my heart with joy as I give back to You.

Help me understand my identity as Your royalty—not a beggar asking for handouts, but a steward managing resources for the richest King. Show me how to give joyfully and faithfully while trusting Your provision.

When old patterns of fear or selfishness surface, remind me of my true identity and generous design. Help me grow in generous living that reflects Your character in a world that needs to see Your love in action.

Free me from the beggar mentality that says I must hoard and scramble. Establish in me the royal identity that trusts You as my Father who delights in providing for His children.

In Jesus' name, Amen.

Key Takeaway

Your identity as God's child makes you royalty—designed to reflect His generous nature, regardless of your financial level. Royal identity means managing resources for the richest King in the universe at whatever level He has entrusted to you.

When you understand your generous design and step into it through trusting obedience, giving becomes a privilege that flows from your DNA, producing joy, peace, and provision that transforms your entire financial experience from beggar's anxiety to royal confidence.

Chapter 2
Choosing Your Master

Carlos couldn't sleep because of his credit card bills. Every night he lay awake calculating payments, interest rates, and minimum balances. Money controlled his thoughts, his mood, and his marriage. Anxiety was consuming his life.

For eighteen months, this had been his routine. Wake up. Panic. Calculate. Promise himself he'd get control. Fall back asleep exhausted. Wake up. Repeat.

"God, I need more money," Carlos prayed desperately.

God's answer surprised him: "Carlos, I don't want your money. I want your heart."

Within six weeks of hearing that answer clearly, Carlos experienced a transformation that amazed his family. His anxiety disappeared, his marriage healed, and provision began flowing into his life through unexpected sources.

But the transformation didn't start with more money. It started with a question Carlos finally let himself ask: *Which master am I actually serving?*

The Spirit Behind the System

Jesus declared something shocking:

> "No one can serve two masters. Either you will hate the one and love the other, or you will be devoted to the one and despise the other. You cannot serve God and Mammon" (Matt. 6:24, NKJV).

Notice Jesus didn't say "money." He said *Mammon*.

Money Isn't the Enemy—Mammon Is

For years, I struggled with confusion about this verse. Bible translations that say "money" instead of "Mammon" can be misleading because money itself is simply a tool—morally neutral, like a hammer or a car.

This confusion gets worse when people misquote Scripture, saying "money is the root of all evil"—implying that money itself is evil and those who have money are somehow less spiritual. But that's not what Scripture says.

Paul actually wrote:

> "The *love* of money is a root of all kinds of evil" (1 Tim. 6:10, emphasis added).

The issue isn't money—it's what we love, what we serve, what we give power to.

Everything changed for me when I read *Wealth, Riches and Money* by Craig Hill and Earl Pitts. They explained that Mammon isn't currency—it's a spiritual power system that seeks to govern our hearts.

Here's the key distinction: It's not about *having* money or *not having* money. It's about the power we ascribe to money—whether we have it or lack it.

Mammon operates equally through:

- The wealthy person who hoards obsessively, fearing loss
- The poor person who obsesses over lack, fearing never having enough
- The middle-class person who calculates anxiously, fearing they're falling behind

The amount in your bank account doesn't determine whether you serve Mammon. The amount of power you give money over your thoughts, decisions, and emotions does.

What Mammon Actually Is

Mammon is more than currency in your wallet or numbers in your account. In the context Jesus uses, Mammon functions as a rival master—a spiritual power system that promises:

- Security without God
- Provision without dependence on Him
- Identity without sonship

Mammon offers independence from God while pretending to meet God-sized needs.

This is why the choice isn't simply about budgeting or financial management.

> "Our struggle is not against flesh and blood, but against... spiritual forces of evil" (Eph. 6:12).

Money itself isn't the enemy. People aren't the enemy. The battle is about who governs the heart.

Mammon operates as a spiritual power seeking authority over:

- **Trust** ("Will God really take care of you?")
- **Obedience** ("Be practical before being faithful.")
- **Fear** ("What if there's not enough?")

That's why Jesus personifies it. You don't "serve" an object—you serve a lord.

Two Voices, Two Kingdoms

> "God is Spirit, and those who worship Him must worship in spirit and truth" (John 4:24).

This matters because:

Mammon governs what is *seen* (numbers, accounts, lack, surplus)

God governs what is *unseen* (His promises, His provision, His timing)

Choosing your master isn't about choosing between generosity and greed—it's about choosing between dependence on a system or dependence on the Spirit. One promises provision without relationship. The other promises provision *through* relationship.

Both voices speak. Both demand allegiance. But they lead to radically different destinations.

Mammon's Voice:

- "Work longer hours to get more of me"
- "Worry about losing me"
- "Make decisions based on accumulating me"
- "Trust me to provide security"

God's Voice:

- "Seek first the kingdom of God, and all these things shall be added to you" (Matt. 6:33)
- "Do not worry about your life, what you will eat or drink" (Matt. 6:25)
- "My God shall supply all your need according to His riches in glory" (Phil. 4:19)
- "The Lord is my shepherd; I shall not want" (Ps. 23:1)

The master you choose shapes the heart you carry—and the heart you carry determines which voice you'll hear when financial decisions arrive.

Carlos's Eighteen-Month Descent

Carlos earned $52,000 annually as a warehouse supervisor—decent income. He and his wife Maria had $8,000 in credit card debt from medical bills two years earlier. The debt wasn't crushing, but for Carlos, it represented failure, shame, and loss of control.

Every decision filtered through one question: *Will this help us pay off the cards faster?*

Maria wanted to visit her mother in Arizona. Too expensive. Their church announced a mission trip to Guatemala. Carlos didn't consider it. When the offering plate passed at church, Carlos typically put in $20. He tithed occasionally—maybe once every two months—when guilt overwhelmed him.

But on most Sundays, he rationalized: *Once we pay off this debt, then I'll be faithful with the tithe. God understands.*

Mammon's voice whispered constantly: *You're not secure. You're failing. Focus on me. Serve me first.*

And Carlos obeyed without question.

The irony? Despite eighteen months of sacrifice and single-minded focus, their $8,000 balance had only decreased to $7,100. Nine hundred dollars in eighteen months.

Meanwhile, Carlos's blood pressure climbed. His marriage grew cold. His relationship with God became nonexistent outside of Sunday attendance.

Mammon promised security if Carlos served it diligently. Instead, Mammon had stolen everything that actually mattered.

The Sermon That Changed Everything

The visiting pastor's message was simple: Every person serves something. The question isn't whether you'll serve—it's *what* you'll serve. Whatever sits on the throne of your life becomes your functional god.

"Some of you serve Mammon," the pastor said. "Here's how you know: Does thinking about finances occupy more mental energy than thinking about God? When you make decisions, does financial impact matter more than spiritual impact?"

Carlos felt his face flush.

"Jesus said you can't serve two masters. Not 'shouldn't serve'—*can't* serve. It's impossible. One will always dominate."

The pastor paused. "So which master do you actually serve? Not which one you *claim* to serve. Which one actually controls your thoughts, your decisions, and your emotional life?"

Carlos knew the answer. He'd been serving Mammon. Faithfully. Diligently. Anxiously.

And Mammon had been a cruel master.

Carlos's Six-Week Transformation

That afternoon, Carlos went for a long walk alone, praying.

"God, I've been serving Mammon. I didn't mean to. I thought I was being responsible. But Mammon has become my master. I'm exhausted. I don't want to live like this anymore."

A thought came with unusual clarity: *Give Me what you've*

been giving to Mammon—your thoughts, your allegiance, your dependence. Start by returning what belongs to Me.

Carlos made a decision that scared him: Starting with his next paycheck, he would return what belonged to God first—the 10% that was holy to Him—$433 monthly. Not when convenient. Not when the debt was paid. First. Every time. Consistently.

This wasn't about being generous. This was about acknowledging whom he was serving.

Mammon had been getting his firstfruits—his attention, his anxiety, his allegiance. God was getting his leftovers. That was backwards.

Week 1: Carlos told Maria about his decision. She looked terrified. "We can barely make debt payments now."

"I know," Carlos admitted. "But serving Mammon hasn't worked. For eighteen months, I've given it everything—and we're miserable. The 10% tithe doesn't belong to us anyway. It's His. I want to try serving God instead of serving our debt."

That Sunday, Carlos nervously wrote the check. But he did it.

On Monday morning at 3 AM, Carlos woke up—but not to calculate bills. He prayed instead. "God, I chose You over Mammon. I acknowledged what belongs to You. Now I'm standing on Your promises to provide."

He fell back asleep peacefully.

Week 2: Mid-week, anxiety returned when Carlos realized they had a $280 electric bill due and only $240 in checking.

His old response would have been panic and obsessive calculation.

Instead, Carlos prayed. "God, I returned what was Yours. Now we need Your provision.

> 'My God shall supply all your need according to His riches in glory by Christ Jesus' (Phil. 4:19)."

Thursday, Maria called from work. Her boss had given her a raise—$50 more per paycheck, $108 monthly.

That evening, their daughter mentioned her school had a program providing free glasses to students who qualified. She'd been selected.

On Friday morning, their church sent an email about a family struggling with medical bills—exactly $500 needed. Carlos felt something unexpected: a prompting to help.

Wait. They didn't have any extra money. They were still paying down debt.

But Carlos realized: The $433 he'd been returning to God—that wasn't his generosity. That was acknowledging God's ownership. If he wanted to be generous, it would be from the remainder God had entrusted to him.

He talked to Maria that evening. "I feel prompted to give $50 to that family."

Maria hesitated. "We're still in debt."

"I know. But the tithe isn't our generosity—that's just returning what's His. This $50 would be different. An offering. Genuine generosity from what He's given us to steward."

They prayed about it. On Saturday morning, Carlos felt at peace. He wrote a second check—$50 to the benevolence fund with the family's name attached.

That act felt different than returning the tithe. The tithe was acknowledgment: "This was never ours." The offering was confidence in God's Word: "What You've given us is enough to be generous with."

Month 2: By month two, Carlos's nightly anxiety sessions had completely stopped. Not because the debt disappeared—they still owed $6,800. But because Mammon was no longer his master.

He and Maria started making different decisions. "What does God want?" replaced "How will this affect our debt payoff?"

When Maria's mother needed help with unexpected car repairs, they gave $200. Not from the tithe—that belonged to God. From the provision God had entrusted to them.

When their church announced the Guatemala missions trip again, Carlos and Maria discussed it. They couldn't afford the $1,800 per person cost. But they felt prompted to give $300 toward scholarships so others could go.

Neither the $200 nor the $300 were the tithe. Those were offerings—generous responses to God's prompting, given from what He'd provided for their household.

The tithe acknowledged God's ownership. The offerings demonstrated their confidence in His continued provision.

Month 3: Three months after that transformative sermon, Carlos sat reviewing their finances with Maria.

The debt had decreased to $6,200—$900 reduction in three months. The same progress it had taken eighteen months to achieve when Mammon was his master.

But everything else had changed:

Their marriage was healing—they prayed together daily

Their daughter was thriving—they said yes to things that mattered

Their giving had increased—$433 monthly tithe plus occasional offerings

Carlos's blood pressure was normal again

The nightly anxiety was permanently gone

"How did this happen?" Maria wondered. "We're giving away more money than before, but we're less anxious and making better progress on the debt."

Carlos knew the answer. "I'm serving a different master. Mammon promised security but delivered slavery. God promises provision and actually delivers it—plus peace, plus joy, plus freedom."

He opened his Bible to Matt. 6:24 and underlined it:

"You cannot serve God and Mammon."

In the margin he wrote: "Tried serving Mammon for 18 months. Nearly destroyed everything. Chose God instead—

returned what's His, relied on Him for the rest. Everything changed."

When Your Whole Life Becomes Worship

> "Therefore, I urge you, brothers and sisters, in view of God's mercy, to offer your bodies as a living sacrifice, holy and pleasing to God—this is your true and proper worship. Do not conform to the pattern of this world, but be transformed by the renewing of your mind. Then you will be able to test and approve what God's will is—his good, pleasing and perfect will" (Rom. 12:1-2).

Paul challenges believers to move beyond compartmentalized religious activities. He calls them to offer their complete selves—everything they are and do—as continuous worship.

Under the New Covenant, God calls you to be a "living sacrifice"—not a dead animal offered once, but a living person offered continuously. Your entire life becomes the offering: daily actions, thoughts, attitudes, work, and relationships.

This is the antidote to serving Mammon: When your whole life becomes worship to God, money returns to its proper place as a tool rather than a master.

Five Ways to Worship Beyond Sunday Morning

When your whole life becomes worship, serving God replaces serving Mammon in every area:

Excellence at Work: David was a mechanic who despised his job until he learned about living sacrifice. He began seeing car repairs as worship through excellence and integrity. His work became ministry, his attitude transformed—not because the job changed, but because he understood fixing cars with excellence honors God.

Patient Parenting: Pamela turned 2 AM feedings into prayer time, offering her exhaustion as worship. Instead of resenting interrupted sleep, she found peace caring for her daughter as an offering to God.

Honest Business Dealings: Jim chose to lose money rather than compromise integrity, seeing ethical business as worship through careful stewardship. His commitment to honesty attracted clients who valued trustworthy contractors.

Kind Customer Service: Ramona saw each difficult customer interaction as opportunity to demonstrate Christ's love through patient service. Her consistently kind responses created a peaceful atmosphere customers noticed. Management promoted her within six months.

Faithful Academic Work: Diana dedicated college studies to God, seeing academic excellence as worship through stewardship of her mind. Her disciplined approach opened scholarship opportunities that provided for her education completely.

Carlos's Complete Transformation

Six weeks became six months. Six months became a year.

Carlos's debt didn't disappear overnight. But it steadily decreased—$7,100 became $5,400 became $3,200.

The difference wasn't dramatically more money. The difference was Carlos no longer served the debt. He served God, and relied on God with the debt.

More importantly, everything else improved:

His marriage—he and Maria prayed together daily, made decisions together, dreamed together. Money was no longer the wedge driving them apart.

His relationship with his daughter—he said yes more often to things that mattered.

His relationship with God—prayer became conversation, worship became authentic, Scripture became living guidance.

His emotional life—nightly anxiety attacks ended permanently. Stress didn't disappear, but Carlos's relationship with stress changed. Mammon's voice no longer controlled his emotional state.

His work—same job, same hours, but work became worship. He served customers with integrity, led his team with wisdom, stewarded his position as service to God.

His giving—the tithe flowed consistently (acknowledging God's ownership), and offerings flowed as prompted (demonstrating confidence in God's provision). Both were worship, but different expressions of it.

One year after that transformative sermon, Carlos sat with his Bible open to Matt. 6:24:

"You cannot serve God and Mammon."

He wrote in the margin: "Serving Mammon: 18 months of anxiety, $900 debt reduction, marriage suffering, God distant. Serving God: 12 months of peace, $3,900 debt reduction, marriage healing, authentic worship. Same income. Different master. Everything changed."

Your Master Choice Creates Your Worship Experience

Every day presents opportunities to choose between serving God or serving Mammon—then living out that choice through how you approach work, relationships, rest, and service.

God doesn't want your money—He wants your heart, your dependence, and your ultimate allegiance.

Your relationship with money should be wise stewardship, using it as a tool for His purposes instead of allowing Mammon's system to control your decisions, emotions, and relationships.

When you place ultimate confidence in God rather than financial security, you break free from Mammon's bondage and align your heart with His desires. Your entire existence becomes continuous worship that connects every moment with His eternal purpose.

Your Call to Choose and Worship

You must choose daily between serving God or serving Mammon—then live out that choice through whole-life worship that demonstrates your allegiance.

When you serve God, money becomes a useful tool for blessing others and building His kingdom. When you serve Mammon, it becomes a demanding master that steals your peace, relationships, and joy.

True worship extends beyond Sunday morning to encompass every aspect of your existence as a living sacrifice to God.

This choice produces peace, unexpected provision, and joy that transcends circumstances.

Carlos discovered that serving God transforms everything. The choice determines not just your financial life, but your entire life.

Which master will you serve?

Questions for Your Heart

1. Which master currently controls most of your financial decisions—God or Mammon?
2. When you examine your thoughts, time, emotions, and decisions—which master do they reveal you're actually serving?
3. What would change if you saw every activity as potential worship to God rather than service to Mammon?

4. What specific step will you take this week to dethrone Mammon and enthrone God?

Prayer for Choosing God and Living Worship

Heavenly Father,

I choose to serve You rather than Mammon and acknowledge You as my ultimate provider and source of security. Help me place complete confidence in You instead of wealth and possessions.

Show me areas where I've been depending on Mammon's system instead of You. Help me return what belongs to You—acknowledging Your ownership, not as obligation but as worship.

Teach me to use what You've entrusted to me wisely and generously for Your kingdom purposes. Help me break free from any bondage to Mammon that controls my decisions or emotions.

When You prompt offerings beyond what belongs to You, give me courage to respond generously, standing on Your promises of continued provision.

Thank You for calling me to present my entire life as a living sacrifice. Help me see work, rest, relationships, and service as opportunities for continuous worship. Make every moment an offering that pleases You.

When I struggle with old patterns of financial anxiety or greed, help me return quickly to serving You. May my heart be fully surrendered, demonstrating Your love and generosity to everyone around me.

Transform my daily activities into worship that honors You and advances Your kingdom through careful stewardship of everything You've entrusted to me.

Let my life be evidence that serving You is better than serving Mammon.

In Jesus' name,

Amen.

Key Takeaway

You must choose daily between serving God or serving Mammon, then live out that choice through whole-life worship that demonstrates your true allegiance. When you serve God—returning to Him what belongs to Him and relying on Him for what He has entrusted to you—money becomes a useful tool for blessing others and building His kingdom, producing peace, unexpected provision, and joy that transform your entire life into continuous worship and careful stewardship. Serving Mammon enslaves you to anxiety, strips your relationships, and costs far more than it ever pays. The tithe acknowledges His ownership; offerings demonstrate your confidence in His provision. Both are worship when you're serving the right Master.

Chapter 3

The Rhythm God Designed

Ethan couldn't stop thinking about the verse he read that morning. Sitting in his dining room with his Bible open to Deuteronomy 14, one phrase had caught his attention:

> "...so that you may learn to revere the LORD your God always."

At 34, married with two kids, Ethan was drowning in anxiety about money. Not because he wasn't working—he had a steady job—but because he was always one emergency away from disaster. Every unexpected expense triggered mental calculation gymnastics: *If we have $1,840 in checking and the car needs $520 in repairs, and rent is $1,200 next week...*

The calculations never stopped. Anxiety never eased.

Then that March morning, reading Deuteronomy 14 during quiet time, verse 23 grabbed him: "...so that you may learn to revere the LORD your God always."

Ethan read it three times. He'd read this passage before, but he'd never noticed that phrase: *so that you may learn to revere.*

Learning to revere. Not instantly revering. Not perfectly revering. *Learning.*

God was saying the tithe is the classroom. Giving firstfruits is how you learn to put Him first in everything else.

Ethan closed his Bible and stared at his checkbook. For 34 years, he'd been learning to fear scarcity. What would it look like to spend the next 34 years learning to revere God instead?

Ethan was about to discover that when you truly hear God and respond in obedience, you unlock a three-phase rhythm that's been working since God first gave it to Israel: Love God with your finances (Heaven), which leads to provision for your household (House), which creates overflow to love your neighbor (Nations).

The question was simple: Would he truly hear by obeying what God was saying about his firstfruits?

When God Gave Clear Instructions About Money

Most Christians assume God stayed silent about finances until Jesus talked about money in the Gospels. But that's not true.

God spoke clearly and specifically to Israel about their finances, establishing a giving system that wasn't complicated —it was intentional. Three distinct rhythms, three specific instructions, three ways to demonstrate that they were listening to His voice:

First:

> "Set aside a tenth of all that your fields produce

> each year. Eat the tithe of your grain, new wine and olive oil, and the firstborn of your herds and flocks in the presence of the LORD your God at the place he will choose as a dwelling for his Name, so that you may learn to revere the LORD your God always" (Deut. 14:22-23).

Every year, bring your firstfruits to worship. Not leftovers. Not what you could spare. The first and best.

Second:

> "At the end of every three years, bring all the tithes of that year's produce and store it in your towns, so that the Levites (who have no allotment or inheritance of their own) and the foreigners, the fatherless and the widows who live in your towns may come and eat and be satisfied" (Deut. 14:28-29).

Every third year, make sure the vulnerable in your community are cared for. The ones who couldn't provide for themselves. The ones society overlooked.

Third:

> "At the end of every seven years you must cancel debts... If anyone is poor among your fellow Israelites in any of the towns of the land the LORD your God is giving you, do not be

> hardhearted or tightfisted toward them. Rather, be openhanded and freely lend them whatever they need... Give generously to them and do so without a grudging heart; then because of this the LORD your God will bless you in all your work and in everything you put your hand to" (Deut. 15:1, 7-8, 10).

Every seven years, practice radical generosity. Cancel debts. Free servants. Open your hand wide to those in need.

Three instructions. Three rhythms. One clear progression.

The Pattern You've Been Living Without Knowing It

Notice what God was teaching through these instructions:

Start with worship - Bring your firstfruits to the place God chooses. This isn't about money. It's about learning to revere Him with everything you have. Your giving demonstrates who you're really listening to: God's voice or fear's whisper.

Trust His provision - "Then because of this the LORD your God will bless you in all your work and in everything you put your hand to." When you honor God first by obeying what He says, He takes responsibility for blessing your household. Not maybe. Not if you're lucky. He promises.

Bless your neighbor - "Do not be hardhearted or tightfisted toward them. Rather, be openhanded." Once you've experienced God's provision in your own house, you have overflow to share with those who need it. You can't give from an empty storehouse, but God doesn't leave His people empty.

Do you see it?

Heaven → House → Nations

Worship Him → Receive from Him → Give to others

Love God →Love yourself rightly → Love your neighbor

This isn't a modern framework someone invented. This is the rhythm God established when He first spoke to His people about their finances. The same God who gave Israel these instructions is speaking to you about your giving today.

Why God Designed the Tithe: Learning to Revere the LORD

Here's the question most people miss: Why did God establish the tithe in the first place?

Read Deut. 14:23 again, slowly:

> "...so that you may learn to revere the LORD your God always."

That phrase is the key to everything. The tithe isn't arbitrary. It's not a religious tax God invented to fund His programs. It's the training ground for something much more foundational: learning proper reverence for God.

The Hebrew word translated "revere" is *yare*—it means to fear, to respect, to hold in awe, to recognize authority. God designed the tithe system to teach His people to put Him first in every area of life, starting with the most tangible, most practical, most anxiety-producing area: money.

Think about it: If you can learn to honor God first with your finances—before the mortgage, before the car payment, before anything else feels secure—you're learning something that transforms everything else. You're learning to recognize His voice as the ultimate authority. You're learning to trust His promises more than your calculations. You're learning what it means to truly hear God by responding in obedience.

The tithe isn't about God needing your money. It's about you needing to learn reverence.

And here's what Scripture promises about that kind of reverence:

> "The fear of the LORD is the beginning of knowledge" (Prov. 1:7).

Do you want to make wise financial decisions? Start with learning to revere God with your finances.

> "The fear of the LORD leads to life; then one rests content, untouched by trouble" (Prov. 19:23).

Want peace about your bills? Learn to put God first, even when your math doesn't work.

> "In the fear of the LORD one has strong confidence, and his children will have a refuge" (Prov. 14:26, ESV).

Do you want security for your household? It comes through learning proper reverence for God, not through hoarding what He's entrusted to you.

The tithe is God's mercy—it's the practical, tangible way He teaches you to trust His voice above every competing authority.

The Alternative: Slavery to Fear of Death

Here's the contrast Scripture draws: You're going to live in fear of something. The question is what?

The writer of Hebrews explains:

> "Since therefore the children share in flesh and blood, he himself likewise partook of the same things, that through death he might destroy the one who has the power of death, that is, the devil, and deliver all those who through fear of death were subject to lifelong slavery" (Heb. 2:14-15, ESV).

Fear of death creates lifelong slavery. Not physical death necessarily—but the fear of not having enough, the fear of running out, the fear that you'll be left destitute if you trust God instead of your own calculations.

That's what controlled Ethan as he sat in his dining room. The fear that if he gave to the Lord first, he'd end up with nothing. The fear that God's math wouldn't work. The fear that trusting His voice would leave him bankrupt.

Jesus came to break that slavery. Not by making the fear disappear instantly, but by giving you a practice—the tithe—that teaches you to recognize His voice as more trustworthy than fear's whisper.

Every time you write that firstfruits check, you're making a declaration: "God, I trust Your voice more than my panic. I believe Your promise to provide. I'm learning to revere You instead of being enslaved to the fear of not having enough."

That's not a religious performance. That's liberation.

Solomon wrote:

> "Better is a little with the fear of the LORD than great treasure and trouble with it" (Prov. 15:16, ESV).

You can have wealth and still be enslaved to fear of death—always calculating, always anxious, always one disaster away from panic. Or you can have less money but live in the freedom that comes from reverence for God—peace that doesn't depend on your bank balance.

The tithe teaches you which fear you're serving: fear of God (reverence, worship, trust) or fear of death (scarcity, anxiety, control).

Ethan's Six-Month Journey: Learning Reverence Through Firstfruits

That Sunday, Ethan wrote his first tithe check before calculating whether his math would work. It felt terrifying. It felt like stepping off a cliff.

It also felt like worship.

Walking to the offering plate, Ethan felt that shift—the sense that he was declaring something true about God's authority over his finances. He wasn't giving out of obligation. He was learning reverence through obedient action.

He'd made his choice. He'd truly heard and now he was obeying. Whatever happened next was in God's hands.

Walking to their car, his wife Melissa squeezed his hand. "How do you feel?"

"Terrified," Ethan admitted. "But also free. Like I finally let God be God."

Months One Through Three

The first few months tested Ethan's resolve. He wrestled daily with his decision. Every bank balance check triggered calculations of what they'd have if he hadn't tithed. The bills got paid, but there was zero margin. Writing the second tithe check felt like bleeding money.

Then the tests came. A car repair emergency. Unexpected dental work for their daughter. The kind of crises that had always triggered Ethan's panic sessions.

But something was different this time. Instead of panic, Ethan prayed. "God, I'm keeping my commitment. Now I'm trusting You."

God's provision came through channels Ethan hadn't planned. His brother helped with the car repair for parts cost, teaching Ethan skills that saved money for years. Melissa's boss announced mid-year bonuses—timing Ethan couldn't predict. Ethan's supervisor offered overtime on a special project.

None of these were dramatic miracles. All of them were provisions that arrived exactly when needed, through means Ethan didn't control.

Month Six: The Transformation

Six months after that March morning with Deuteronomy, Ethan and Melissa reviewed their finances. Their income had increased by about $600 monthly through various provisions —more than their monthly tithe.

But the real transformation wasn't the numbers. It was what had shifted inside Ethan. The anxiety that had characterized his relationship with money for five years was... gone. Not because they had dramatically more money, but because the rhythm had established peace.

Heaven first: They were worshiping God consistently through firstfruits giving.

House second: They were experiencing His provision for their household through unexpected channels.

Nations next: For the first time, they started to think beyond their own needs.

Ethan opened his Bible to Deut. 14:23 and added a note in the margin: "August: Six months of learning to revere God through firstfruits giving. He's provided every step. The rhythm is real: Heaven → House → Nations."

The Holy Distinction: What the Tithe Teaches You

Here's something crucial about learning reverence: You must learn to distinguish between what's holy and what's common.

> "A tithe of everything from the land, whether grain from the soil or fruit from the trees, belongs to the LORD; it is holy to the LORD" (Lev. 27:30).

The tithe doesn't become holy because you give it. It's holy already—it belongs to God. When you tithe, you're not making something sacred; you're acknowledging what was already sacred and returning what was always His.

That's a radically different way of thinking about money.

Most people think: "I earned this money. Then I decide to give some to God." But Scripture says: "The first tenth was never yours. It's holy—set apart—belonging to God. When you tithe, you're learning to recognize that distinction."

God told the priests:

> "You must distinguish between the holy and the common, between the unclean and the clean" (Lev. 10:10).

That's what the tithe teaches you to do with finances. You learn to see money differently—not as all the same, but as having distinctions.

The first tenth is holy. It belongs to the Lord. Learning to treat it as such—releasing it before you touch anything else—that's how you learn about reverence.

When you blur that line—when you treat the tithe as "optional" or "something I'll do if there's enough left over"—you're not just making a financial decision. You're demonstrating that you haven't learned to distinguish holy from common. You haven't learned proper reverence.

The tithe is God's mercy: it's the tangible, practical way He teaches you to see His ownership over everything, starting with the most concrete 10%.

Your Invitation to the Rhythm

God isn't asking you to invent a new approach to finances. He's inviting you to embrace the rhythm He designed when He first spoke to His people about giving:

This week, honor Him with firstfruits—give before you pay anything else, demonstrating that you're listening to His voice about your finances and learning to revere Him above your fears.

This month, trust His promise to bless the work of your hands —watch for provision that comes through means you didn't calculate or coordinate.

This season, be openhanded toward your neighbors—look for practical ways to bless those in your community who need help.

The same God who established this rhythm for Israel is speaking to you about your giving today. The question isn't whether His rhythm works. The question is whether you'll truly hear His instructions—not just listen to them but obey them and begin the journey of learning reverence.

Heaven → House → Nations.

Worship → Provision → Generosity.

Love God → Love yourself rightly → Love your neighbor.

Fear of the Lord → Freedom from fear of death → Confidence to bless others.

It's not a new idea. It's what God's been saying all along.

The rhythm that worked for Israel still works today. The rhythm that transformed Ethan's anxiety can transform your relationship with money.

God designed you to live in this rhythm. Your generous life—the life of freedom, peace, and purposeful giving—awaits your first step of obedience.

The rhythm begins when you stop merely listening and start truly hearing—responding to God's voice with obedient action. And the tithe is where you learn what reverence actually looks like in practice.

> "The fear of the LORD is a fountain of life,
> turning a person from the snares of death"
> (Prov. 14:27).

That fountain begins flowing when you write your first firstfruits check.

Questions for Your Heart

1. Have you been listening to God's voice about finances, or truly hearing in a way that leads to obedience and learning reverence?
2. Which fear is louder in your financial decisions: reverence for God or fear of not having enough?
3. What would change if you viewed the tithe not as God taking from you, but as God teaching you to distinguish between holy and common?
4. What practical step will you take this week to begin learning reverence through firstfruits giving?

Prayer for Learning Reverence

Heavenly Father, thank You for not leaving me to figure out finances on my own. You spoke clearly to Israel about giving, and You're speaking clearly to me today through Your Word.

Help me not just listen to Your voice but truly hear it—responding in obedience to what You're saying about my finances. I want to learn reverence, starting with my wallet. Teach me to distinguish between what's holy and what's common. Help me see that the tithe isn't You taking from me, but You teaching me to trust Your voice above my fear.

Give me courage to write the firstfruits check even when my math doesn't seem to work. Help me remember that You designed the tithe to teach me reverence, not to burden me. You're breaking my slavery to fear of death and teaching me the freedom that comes from proper fear of You.

Thank You that learning reverence is a process. Thank You for patience as I take these first steps of obedience. Show me this month how You bless the work of my hands when I honor You first. Let me experience the truth that the fear of the LORD is a fountain of life.

Move me from merely listening to truly hearing—from knowing what You say to doing what You say. Let obedience to Your voice about firstfruits unlock the rhythm You designed: Heaven, then House, then Nations.

In Jesus' name, Amen.

Key Takeaway

God designed the tithe to teach you reverence—to break your slavery to fear of death and train you to trust His voice above financial anxiety. The rhythm He established thousands of years ago still works today: worship Him with firstfruits (Heaven), trust His promise to bless the work of your hands (House), then be openhanded toward neighbors in need (Nations). The Hebrew word for "hear" (*shema*) means both listening and obeying—they're inseparable. When you truly hear God's voice about finances by responding in obedience rather than merely listening to teaching, you begin learning proper reverence. And reverence, Scripture promises, is "a fountain of life" (Prov. 14:27)

that protects you from the snares of financial fear and positions you for the generous life God designed.

Chapter 4
God's Kingdom Economics

Bennett had been earning six figures and tithing faithfully for three years. He gave 10% to his church every month. He donated to multiple charities. He supported missionaries. On paper, his financial obedience looked flawless.

But despite doing everything "right," anxiety consumed him.

He couldn't sleep at night. Every market downturn triggered panic. Every unexpected expense felt like a crisis. His bank account was impressive. His heart felt empty and anxious.

Bennett's wife, Lauren, finally confronted him one Saturday morning after he'd spent an hour obsessing over their investment portfolio. "You're tithing faithfully. You're giving generously. But you're not at peace. What's actually controlling you—God or money?"

The question hit hard.

Bennett realized something powerful that morning: He'd been giving from obligation while seeking first his own financial security. His heart was divided between kingdom priorities and maintaining his lifestyle. He was performing financial obedience while trusting his investments more than God.

Over the next nine months, Bennett discovered that God doesn't operate on human economic principles. When you seek His kingdom first—really first, with your whole heart—His provision works through mathematics that defy calculation.

But it took a crisis to teach him.

The First Person Who Ever Gave a Tithe

Nobody commanded Abraham to tithe. No law had yet existed. No religious system told him it was required.

Abraham had just won a dangerous battle against multiple kings who had kidnapped his nephew Lot. On his journey home, exhausted and victorious, he met Melchizedek, king of Salem and priest of God Most High.

> "Then Melchizedek king of Salem brought out bread and wine. He was priest of God Most High, and he blessed Abram, saying, 'Blessed be Abram by God Most High, Creator of heaven and earth. And praise be to God Most High, who delivered your enemies into your hand.' Then Abram gave him a tenth of everything" (Gen. 14:18-20).

Abraham gave out of pure gratitude. He recognized God as his source of victory and provision. This wasn't religious duty—it was worship flowing from a heart that understood kingdom economics.

Think about the context: Abraham was wealthy. He'd just recovered substantial plunder from defeated kings. He could have kept everything and become even richer. Instead, he gave the first tenth to God's priest as an act of reverence.

Abraham understood something powerful: Everything he possessed came from God's blessing, not his own strength. When you truly grasp that truth, giving becomes natural worship rather than a reluctant obligation.

Centuries later, God formalized what Abraham discovered instinctively:

> "Be sure to set aside a tenth of all that your fields produce each year... so that you may learn to revere the LORD your God always" (Deut. 14:22-23).

The tithe isn't about God needing your money. It's about you learning what Abraham already knew: proper reverence for God—the fear of the Lord—transforms how you see everything you possess.

Why This Ancient Story Still Matters for Your Finances

The writer of Hebrews explains why Abraham's encounter with Melchizedek matters for us today:

> "Just think how great he was: Even the patriarch Abraham gave him a tenth of the plunder!... In the one case, the tenth is collected by people who die; but in the other case, by him who is declared to be living" (Heb. 7:4, 8).

Melchizedek was a preview of Jesus Christ, serving as priest forever. When we tithe faithfully, we're following Abraham's example, recognizing that Christ our eternal High Priest is worthy of our worship through generous giving.

Tithing transcends Old Testament law—it's worship that continues under Jesus Christ's eternal priesthood. Abraham gave centuries before the law. We give centuries after the law. The principle remains: God deserves our firstfruits because He is our ultimate provider.

Seek First the Kingdom—Watch What Happens

Jesus gave us the operating principle for kingdom economics:

> "But seek first his kingdom and his righteousness, and all these things will be given to you as well" (Matt. 6:33).

This isn't spiritual advice for Sunday mornings. This is practical guidance for managing everything in your daily life—including money, career, relationships, and priorities.

Notice what Jesus doesn't say: "Seek first the kingdom and His blessings." He says, "seek first the kingdom and His righteousness."

Righteousness comes first. Peace follows naturally. The provision arrives through channels you didn't arrange.

Bennett discovered this truth the hard way.

Bennett's Nine-Month Journey

Month One - March: Bennett sat in his financial advisor's office reviewing his portfolio. Everything looked good on paper. Retirement accounts are growing. Investment properties are appreciating. Emergency fund fully funded.

But Bennett felt sick inside. The anxiety wasn't decreasing as his net worth increased—it was getting worse.

That evening, he confessed to Lauren: "I've been seeking first my financial security, not God's kingdom. I give my tithe, but I'm trusting my portfolio more than I'm trusting God."

Lauren was quiet for a moment, then: "So what would change if you actually sought God's kingdom first?"

Bennett didn't have an answer.

Month Two - April: Bennett started praying differently. Instead of his usual morning prayer—"God, bless my finances, protect my investments, help me make wise decisions"—he prayed: "God, I want to seek Your kingdom first. Not my financial security. Not my comfort. Not my retirement timeline. Your kingdom. Show me what that means."

Nothing dramatic happened. But Bennett felt that shift—a loosening of the death grip he'd had on his financial security.

Month Three - May: The test came.

Bennett's church announced a partnership with a ministry rescuing trafficking survivors.

The vision: to build a restoration center that provides long-term care for 20 women annually.

The need: $3 million over three years for facility, staff, and programs.

The recommended pledge? Three years of proportional giving above the tithe.

Bennett ran the numbers. For his income level, they suggested $25,000 annually for three years. Total: $75,000.

The old Bennett would have immediately calculated what that would cost: delayed retirement by how many months? Reduced vacation budget by what percentage? Postponed investment property purchase for how long?

But something had shifted. Bennett heard God's voice clearly during the pledge service: "Seek My kingdom first. Trust Me with your finances."

Bennett wrote down $25,000 annually for three years. His hand trembled. Lauren squeezed his arm.

Walking to their car after the service, Lauren asked: "How do you feel?"

"Terrified," Bennett admitted. "But also, more at peace than I've felt in years. I think I just chose which master I'm actually serving."

Months Four Through Nine: The provision didn't come how Bennett expected.

No windfall appeared. No unexpected inheritance. There is no dramatic increase in salary.

Instead, God's mathematics worked differently:

His priorities shifted—Bennett realized he'd been spending $800 monthly on things that didn't matter. Magazine subscriptions he never read. Streaming services he rarely watched. Premium versions of apps he didn't need. A gym membership he hadn't used in months. When he canceled these things, he suddenly had $800 monthly he didn't know was being wasted.

His contentment increased—Before seeking God's kingdom first, Bennett constantly compared his possessions to his neighbors'. After the shift, he found genuine satisfaction with what he had. The anxiety about needing more disappeared.

His generosity multiplied—Something happened in Bennett's heart. Giving stopped feeling like a sacrifice and started feeling like worship. He found himself looking for opportunities to bless others, not because he had to, but because he wanted to.

The promised pledge? Fully funded through the three years—not because Bennett's income dramatically increased, but because seeking God's kingdom first changed what Bennett wanted, what Bennett needed, and how Bennett saw his resources.

Nine months later, Bennett told his small group, "For three years, I tithed faithfully while trusting my portfolio more than God. I was giving to the kingdom while seeking first my own security. When I truly began seeking God's kingdom first—when my heart aligned with His righteousness rather than my comfort—everything changed. Not my income. My heart."

This is the difference between tithing from duty and seeking God's kingdom first. You can write the checks mechanically while your heart remains enslaved to the fear of death. Or you can write them as acts of worship, learning reverence by honoring God first.

The tithe trains you in proper fear. But only when your heart is genuinely seeking His kingdom, not just performing religious obligations.

The Three Things That Actually Satisfy

Paul explains what God's kingdom offers that money cannot purchase:

> "For the kingdom of God is not a matter of eating and drinking, but of righteousness, peace and joy in the Holy Spirit" (Rom. 14:17).

These three realities satisfy in ways bank accounts never can:

Righteousness: Living aligned with God's will and character. When you seek God's kingdom first, your life aligns with His purposes. You experience the satisfaction of knowing you're living according to how you were designed.

Peace: Freedom from anxiety about circumstances. Bennett had a six-figure income but no peace. The difference? He sought financial security first instead of God's kingdom first.

Joy: Deep contentment that difficult circumstances cannot disturb. This isn't happiness dependent on situations going well. It's joy rooted in relationship with God and participation in His kingdom work—joy that persists even when your portfolio decreases or unexpected bills arrive.

When you focus on these three spiritual realities, you find satisfaction that transcends what money can purchase. And here's the remarkable promise: When you seek first God's kingdom and these three things, Jesus says "all these things will be given to you as well."

The provision follows. The needs get met. But through channels you didn't calculate or control.

How God's Mathematics Actually Work

God operates on economics that defy human logic. His provision doesn't follow the formulas you learned in business school or from your financial advisor.

Solomon wrote:

> "Honor the LORD with your wealth, with the firstfruits of all your crops; then your barns will be filled to overflowing, and your vats will brim over with new wine" (Prov. 3:9-10).

Notice the sequence:

1. Honor God FIRST (tithe before bills, seek His kingdom before your security)
2. God fills your barns (provision follows obedience)

Not maybe. Not if you're lucky. Not if market conditions are favorable. God promises it.

But here's what most people miss: God's provision doesn't

always look like more money appearing in your account. His mathematics work through multiple channels:

- **Opened eyes** - You see provision you were missing (Bennett discovered $800 monthly in wasted spending)
- **Perfect timing** - Opportunities arrive exactly when needed
- **Changed priorities** - You need less because you want different things (contentment replaces constant upgrade mentality)
- **Increased wisdom** - You steward better what you already have
- **Community provision** - People share resources you didn't know were available
- **Supernatural peace** - Anxiety lifts even before circumstances change

God's math isn't just about multiplication of money. It's about multiplication of provision through every channel He controls —which is all of them.

My Personal Discovery: When $18,500 Was More Than Enough

I need to tell you how I learned this truth personally.

My wife and I were earning $18,500 annually combined income with two young boys. That's not a typo—less than $20,000 in total household income. Every month brought more bills than income.

Then I heard a sermon about tithing that challenged everything I believed about finances. The pastor read Malachi 3:10: "'Bring the whole tithe into the storehouse, that there may be food in my house. Test me in this,' says the LORD Almighty, 'and see if I will not throw open the floodgates of heaven and pour out so much blessing that there will not be room enough to store it.'"

My first thought: "Ten percent to God when we barely have 100% for ourselves? That's financial suicide."

But something stirred in my heart—that quiet voice I'd learned to recognize as God speaking. I felt Him say: "Trust Me. Test My promise. See if My mathematics work."

I went home and told my wife what I'd heard. I expected resistance. Instead, she said: "I've been feeling the same thing. Let's trust God's Word for three months."

We calculated our tithe: 10% of our gross income, about $154 monthly. That doesn't sound like much, but when you're earning $18,500 annually, $154 feels like a fortune. We wrote the check that first month with trembling hands.

Over those three months, God's mathematics proved reliable. Not through dramatic windfalls, but through opened eyes—we realized we'd been wasting money on convenience foods and started cooking from scratch, cutting our grocery budget significantly. Through changed priorities—contentment replaced constant comparison with wealthier friends. Through supernatural peace—the 3 AM anxiety about finances lifted even before our circumstances dramatically improved.

By the end of three months, we were convinced: The 90% with God's blessing went further than 100% without it.

Thirty years later, I can testify with complete confidence: God's mathematics have never failed us. Not once. Did we always see dramatic provisions? No. Did bills sometimes come due before money had arrived? Yes. Did we face financial pressure? Absolutely.

But honoring God first with firstfruits giving positioned us to experience provision we could not have organized. The 90% with God's blessing consistently went further than 100% ever would have without it.

We learned what Abraham knew instinctively: When you recognize God as your ultimate provider and honor Him first with your finances, you're not giving up security—you're gaining access to kingdom economics that defy human calculation.

Common Questions About Kingdom Economics

"I Can't Afford to Tithe"

The biblical truth: You can't afford NOT to tithe.

When you honor God first with firstfruits giving, He makes your remaining money work in supernatural ways. Not through magic, but through kingdom economics that operate on principles you can't calculate or control.

I couldn't afford to tithe on $18,500 annually—until I did and discovered God's mathematics work. Bennett couldn't afford to pledge $75,000 to the cause of rescuing trafficking survivors—until he did and found that seeking God's kingdom first changed what he needed and wanted.

"Should I Pay Bills First or Tithe First?"

God asks for firstfruits, not leftovers.

> "Honor the LORD with your wealth, with the firstfruits of all your crops; then your barns will be filled to overflowing" (Prov. 3:9-10).

Notice: Honor Him FIRST. Then the barns fill. Not the other way around.

If you wait until all bills are paid, there's never anything left. But when you honor God first by giving before paying anything else, He takes responsibility for making the rest work.

"What If My Circumstances Don't Change?"

Tithing is worship that builds faith, teaches trust, and aligns your heart with His kingdom priorities. The greatest change often happens in your heart first, then your circumstances.

Bennett's income didn't dramatically increase, but his anxiety disappeared when he started seeking God's kingdom first. I didn't get a raise after tithing on $18,500, but the 90% went further than 100% ever had.

Make no mistake—when you consistently honor God with the tithe, things change. His math always works. But it works through kingdom economics that defy your calculations, not through predictable formulas you can control.

Your Invitation to Kingdom Economics

God isn't asking you to trust your own calculations. He's inviting you to test His mathematics—to discover that when you seek first His kingdom and His righteousness, provision follows through channels you don't devise.

Abraham learned this truth four thousand years ago when he gave a tenth to Melchizedek. I learned it thirty years ago on $18,500 annually. Bennett learned it nine months ago at six figures. The income level doesn't matter—kingdom economics work every time regardless of income.

This week, make the choice:

- Will you seek first God's kingdom, or will you seek first your own financial security?
- Will you honor Him with firstfruits, or will you give Him leftovers after your bills feel secure?
- Will you trust His mathematics, or will you rely on your own calculations?

The same God who provided for Abraham is speaking to you about your giving today. The same God who made my $18,500 work is promising to make your finances work through kingdom economics.

The rhythm that God established in Deuteronomy still functions today: Learn to revere the Lord through firstfruits giving (Heaven), trust His promise to bless the work of your hands (House), then be openhanded toward your neighbors from the overflow He creates (Nations).

It starts with seeking first His kingdom. It continues through honoring Him first with your finances. It results in experiencing provision through mathematics you didn't calculate but can absolutely trust.

Your generous life—the life of righteousness, peace, and joy that transcends your bank balance—awaits your first step of obedience.

Questions for Your Heart

1. Are you seeking first God's kingdom or your own financial security? What does your bank statement reveal about which one you're actually prioritizing?
2. Have you been giving from duty while trusting your portfolio more than God? What would change if you truly sought His kingdom first?
3. Which of the three things that satisfy—righteousness, peace, or joy—are you missing because you're seeking security instead of God's kingdom?
4. What practical step will you take this week to begin trusting God's kingdom economics instead of your own calculations?

Prayer for Kingdom Living

Heavenly Father, thank You for the peace that comes from seeking Your kingdom and Your righteousness first.

I confess I've been seeking first my own financial security while giving You leftovers instead of firstfruits. I've been tithing from obligation while trusting my investments more than Your promises. Forgive me for my divided heart.

Help me seek first Your kingdom in every financial decision. Let my heart align with Your righteousness, not my comfort. Give me courage to test Your mathematics—to honor You first even when my calculations don't seem to work.

I choose to trust Your kingdom economics over my own calculations. I believe that when I seek first Your kingdom, You'll add "all these things" to my life. Give me the three things that truly satisfy: righteousness, peace, and joy in the Holy Spirit.

Move me from seeking first my security to seeking first Your kingdom. Let me experience the provision that comes through channels I don't control but can absolutely trust.

In Jesus' name, Amen.

Key Takeaway

God's kingdom operates on economics that defy human calculation—when you genuinely seek first His kingdom and righteousness instead of your own financial security, provision follows through channels you don't orchestrate but can trust completely. Abraham discovered this truth when he gave the first tithe four thousand years ago; it still works today at every income level. The 90% with God's blessing always goes further than 100% without it, not through magic but through kingdom mathematics: opened eyes, perfect timing, changed priorities, increased wisdom, community provision, and supernatural peace. When you seek first God's kingdom, He provides the three things that truly satisfy—righteousness, peace, and joy—plus "all these things" you need, working through provision you cannot calculate but can absolutely trust.

Chapter 5

Following Spiritual Feeding

Shandel was confused about where to give her tithe.

Her old church said tithe to the building fund. Her new church said tithe wherever you get spiritually fed. Her friend insisted it didn't matter because "we're under grace."

"Who's right?" Shandel wondered. "And why does it matter where I give?"

Shandel was about to discover that following this simple principle would revolutionize not just her giving, but her entire spiritual life.

How Tithing Worked in the Old Testament

In the Old Testament, God established the Levitical priesthood to serve in the Tabernacle and temple. As priests, they had no land inheritance or business opportunities. Instead, God provided for them through the people's tithes.

> "I give to the Levites all the tithes in Israel as their inheritance in return for the work they do while serving at the tent of meeting... The Levites will receive no inheritance among the Israelites" (Num. 18:21, 23b, paraphrased).

The concept is further explained:

> "The Levitical priests—indeed, the whole tribe of Levi—are to have no allotment or inheritance with Israel. They shall live on the food offerings presented to the LORD, for that is their inheritance" (Deut. 18:1, ESV).

The tithe's purpose was supporting those who fed God's people spiritually—teaching His Word, facilitating worship, and helping people understand His ways. Tithes went to those who nourished souls and built faith.

The principle was simple: Your tithe supports those who feed you spiritually.

Why Jesus Changes Everything About Tithing

When Jesus came, He became our eternal High Priest in the order of Melchizedek—not temporary like the Levites, but permanent and perfect (see Heb. 7:1-3).

Melchizedek received Abraham's tithe because of the spiritual truth and blessing Abraham experienced through his ministry. Abraham tithed because of the spiritual feeding he received.

As believers today, we tithe not from law but from grace, following Abraham's example. The principle remains: Support those who feed you spiritually and help you grow in your relationship with Jesus.

Firstfruits Giving Trains You in Reverence

Remember why God established the tithe in the first place:

> "...so that you may learn to revere the LORD your God always" (Deut. 14:22-23).

The practice of giving firstfruits—whether to your local church, an online ministry, or multiple sources that feed you—isn't just about funding programs. It's about training yourself in proper fear of the Lord. It's the tangible, practical way you learn to put God first in every area of life.

When you write that firstfruits check to wherever is genuinely feeding your soul, you're making a declaration: "God, I trust Your voice more than my anxiety. I believe spiritual feeding matters more than institutional loyalty. I'm learning to revere You by supporting what actually nourishes my relationship with You."

The Biblical Default: Your Local Church

Before we go further, let's establish the foundation clearly: Your local church should be your primary source of spiritual nourishment. God designed the body of Christ to feed, challenge, and mature you through consistent teaching, community, and accountability. This is the biblical default—not a suggestion you can ignore when convenient.

The writer of Hebrews instructs:

> "And let us consider how we may spur one another on toward love and good deeds, not

> giving up meeting together, as some are in the habit of doing, but encouraging one another—and all the more as you see the Day approaching" (Heb. 10:24-25).

Your local church provides something no online ministry, podcast, or book can fully replace: physical presence, face-to-face community, local accountability, tangible service opportunities, and shepherds who know your name and circumstances.

If your local church is feeding you spiritually—teaching Scripture faithfully, challenging you to grow, deepening your relationship with God—then that's where your tithe should flow with gratitude and joy.

But what happens when your soul stops growing there?

From Milk to Meat: God-Directed Development

Just as a nursing mother provides what her infant needs, your local church should nourish your early growth in faith. A baby depends entirely on their mother's milk for survival. It's perfect nutrition for that stage of development.

But infants don't stay on milk forever.

The writer of Hebrews rebuked believers for exactly this issue:

> "In fact, though by this time you ought to be teachers, you need someone to teach you the elementary truths of God's word all over again. You need milk, not solid food! Anyone

> who lives on milk, being still an infant, is not acquainted with the teaching about righteousness. But solid food is for the mature, who by constant use have trained themselves to distinguish good from evil" (Heb. 5:12-14).

Notice the progression: milk for infants, meat for the mature. God expects growth. He expects development. Sometimes staying comfortable in elementary teaching is actually stunting your spiritual growth.

There comes a time when God transitions you from milk to meat, directing you to teaching that challenges you at a deeper level because He's calling you to maturity. This isn't abandoning the local church—it's recognizing that God feeds you as He develops you.

The key distinction: This is God-directed development, not consumer preference. There's a massive difference between God calling you to deeper feeding and you avoiding difficult truths.

What This Is NOT

Let's be brutally honest: wounded people often confuse their offense with God's direction. You didn't hear God tell you to leave—you heard your pride tell you to run.

This principle about following spiritual feeding is NOT:

An excuse to leave because you're hurt or offended. If your pastor challenged your lifestyle, confronted your sin, or held you accountable—and that's why you're considering leaving—you're not following spiritual feeding. You're running from correction.

Permission to church-hop based on preference or conflict. If you've left three churches in five years, the problem might not be the churches. It might be you. Serial church-hoppers share a common pattern: they blame the church for not feeding them, but what they really mean is the church stopped entertaining them or started challenging them.

Freedom to chase after popular teachers randomly. The most entertaining preacher isn't necessarily the one God wants feeding you. Depth matters more than charisma. Challenge matters more than comfort.

License to avoid difficult seasons or hard truths. Sometimes the teaching that feeds your soul most is the teaching that confronts your comfortable theology, challenges your lifestyle, or exposes blind spots you didn't know you had.

If you've left multiple churches, always blaming them for not "feeding" you, the problem isn't the churches. It's you.

The Accountability Framework

The Deuteronomy passage that establishes tithing specifies

"the place the LORD will choose" (Deut. 14:23).

Not the place that entertains you. Not the place that flatters you. The place God chooses.

Wherever you're being fed—whether local church, online ministry, or other sources—it must include three non-negotiable elements:

Assembly: You cannot be spiritually fed in isolation.

> "And let us consider how we may spur one another on toward love and good deeds, not giving up meeting together" (Heb. 10:24-25).

Spiritual feeding happens in community, not as a consumer in an audience.

Accountability: Feeding without accountability produces consumers, not disciples. You need people who know you, challenge you, and hold you responsible for growth.

> "As iron sharpens iron, so one person sharpens another" (Prov. 27:17).

Biblical Alignment: Teaching must square with Scripture, not just sound appealing. The Bereans

> "received the message with great eagerness and examined the Scriptures every day to see if what Paul said was true" (Acts 17:11).

Notice: all three elements require more than passive consumption. Assembly means showing up. Accountability means being known. Biblical alignment means testing everything against Scripture.

How to Discern the Difference

So how do you know if God is directing you to new feeding sources or if you're just running from correction?

Ask yourself these questions with brutal honesty:

God-Directed Transition:

- Has your local church fed you well for a season, and now you're sensing a call to deeper teaching that challenges you at a new level?
- Are you leaving toward something God is clearly directing, not away from something that hurt you?
- Have you sought counsel from mature believers who know you well and can speak objectively about your patterns?
- Can you articulate what specific area God is developing in you that requires different feeding?
- Are you pursuing assembly and accountability in the new place, not just consuming content?

Reactionary Church-Hopping:

- Are you leaving because of conflict, offense, or hurt feelings?
- Is this your pattern—leaving churches when challenged or uncomfortable?

- Are you chasing popular teachers or big-name ministries rather than seeking depth?
- Would you describe yourself as a "consumer" seeking the best experience rather than a servant committed to a community?
- Did you leave your last church because of a conflict? And the one before that?

If you answer yes to most questions in the first category, God may genuinely be directing you to new feeding sources. If you answer 'yes' to most in the second category, you're not following spiritual feeding. You're following your wounded ego away from the very accountability God wants to use to mature you.

David's Journey: From Loyalty to Feeding

David moved to a new city for work. He visited several churches and settled on one that seemed friendly. Good people. Active programs. Welcoming atmosphere.

He started attending regularly and began tithing faithfully.

Month three, David sat in his usual pew on Sunday morning. The sermon was about being positive and believing in yourself. Nice thoughts. Encouraging words. But nothing that challenged him spiritually or taught him something new about God's character.

He'd heard similar messages the previous eight Sundays.

That afternoon, David listened to a Bible teaching podcast while doing yard work. The teacher was walking through Romans 8, verse by verse, explaining the Greek words, connecting Old Testament prophecies, showing how everything pointed to Christ.

David stopped raking. He rewound and listened again. Something awakened in his spirit—hunger for depth, for substance, for teaching that actually fed his soul.

Over the next month, David realized something uncomfortable: He was learning more from a forty-minute podcast than from months of Sunday sermons.

The Wrestling Period

"Should I tithe to my local church out of loyalty," David wondered, "or to the ministry actually feeding me?"

The guilt was real. These were good people at his church. They'd welcomed him. The pastor was kind.

But kindness wasn't the same as spiritual feeding.

For three weeks, David wrestled with these questions. He kept tithing to his local church out of obligation, but the joy was gone.

David also examined his own heart carefully. Was this about wanting entertainment? Was he running from something the pastor had said that convicted him? He reviewed the last three months of sermons honestly. No offense. No conflict. No avoidance. Just genuine spiritual hunger for deeper teaching.

The Prayer Decision

One evening, David sat with his Bible and journal. "God, I need wisdom. I want to honor You with my tithe, but I also want to support ministry that's actually feeding my soul. Show me what to do."

Over the next week, two passages kept arresting his attention:

> "My sheep listen to my voice; I know them, and they follow me" (John 10:27).

Where was he hearing Jesus' voice most clearly? Through the podcast teaching that unpacked Scripture verse by verse.

> "Nevertheless, the one who receives instruction in the word should share all good things with their instructor" (Gal. 6:6).

Paul said to support those who teach you the Word. The podcast teacher was teaching him Scripture. His local church pastor was giving motivational talks.

David decided: He would redirect his tithe to the podcast ministry that was transforming his biblical understanding. He would still attend his local church and serve there, but his tithe would follow the feeding.

The Timeline of Transformation

The first month after redirecting his tithe: David felt a weight lift. Writing that check to the podcast ministry felt like worship instead of obligation. He started taking notes during the teaching. His prayer life shifted from vague requests to specific prayers based on Scripture he was learning.

Third month: David's wife noticed the change. "You're different," she said one evening. "You've been talking about the Bible more. You seem... I don't know... more grounded."

David had started a morning routine: coffee, Bible, and listening to the podcast teaching. Passages he'd read for years suddenly made sense. Doctrines he'd never understood clicked into place.

Six months later: David felt prompted to start a Bible study at work. Three coworkers were interested. David used the same verse-by-verse method he'd been learning from the podcast.

The group grew to eight people. Two of them weren't believers when they started. Both gave their lives to Christ after six months of studying Scripture together.

One year after the decision: David could barely recognize his spiritual life from twelve months earlier. His biblical knowledge had expanded dramatically. His prayer life had depth and confidence. He was teaching Scripture to others and seeing lives transformed.

"When I started supporting where I was actually getting fed," David told his men's group, "my spiritual life exploded with growth. God honored my decision to follow the feeding principle. I'm not against my local church—I still serve there. But my tithe goes where my soul gets fed, and that decision changed everything."

Lydia's Rural Challenge: Geography vs. Feeding

Lydia lived three hours from any substantial church. Her small town had one congregation—thirty people on a good Sunday, led by a part-time pastor who worked construction during the week.

The sermons were simple. Sometimes encouraging. Often repetitive. Lydia had heard the same messages multiple times over her five years there.

She loved the people. She served faithfully. But her soul was starving.

The Discovery

A friend mentioned an online church offering live Sunday services, midweek Bible studies via video call, and pastoral care through video meetings. Lydia visited the website skeptically.

"This can't be real church," she thought. "You need a physical presence. You need a community."

But curiosity won. Lydia attended an online Sunday service.

The teaching was deep. The worship was powerful. The Scripture exposition was thorough and clear. For the first time in years, Lydia felt spiritually fed.

She started attending regularly online while still showing up at her local church building. Within weeks, she joined an online small group that met via video every Wednesday evening. Eight people from different states studying Scripture together.

Lydia's soul came alive.

The Criticism

When Lydia mentioned to a local church member that she was participating in an online church, the response was immediate and harsh.

"That's not a real church, Lydia. You can't just abandon us."

"I'm not abandoning anyone," Lydia tried to explain. "I'm still here every Sunday. I'm still serving. I just—"

"You're stealing from us. That tithe belongs to your local church."

The criticism stung. Over the next month, three different people confronted Lydia about "abandoning her community" and "chasing after false teaching."

The Wrestling and Resolution

Lydia lay awake several nights wrestling with doubt. "Am I behaving selfishly? Am I abandoning my community?"

She examined her heart carefully. Was she leaving because she was offended? No—she still loved these people and continued serving them. Was she running from accountability? No—she was pursuing more accountability through the online small group that met weekly and knew about her struggles intimately.

Lydia realized something crucial: God had been feeding her faithfully through her local church for years, but He was now calling her to meat when she'd been sustained on milk. This wasn't abandonment—it was development.

She redirected her tithe to the online ministry while continuing to serve her local church.

Two Years Later

By the end of the first year, Lydia was meeting with three women from her community for Bible study. Word spread that "Lydia knows the Bible." People started asking her questions about passages. The local pastor even asked her to teach a women's Bible study.

Year Two: The women's Bible study grew to fifteen women. Some drove from neighboring towns. Lives were being transformed. Women who had attended church for decades were understanding Scripture for the first time.

"For the first six months, I wondered if I'd made a terrible mistake," Lydia told a friend two years later. "Nothing visible changed. The criticism continued. I questioned my decision constantly.

"But I kept following the feeding principle—supporting the ministry that was actually feeding my soul. And God used that spiritual growth to transform not just me, but my entire community.

"The people who criticized me now benefit from the teaching I'm able to give because I followed spiritual feeding instead of institutional loyalty."

Practical Guidelines for Modern Tithing

If your local pastor feeds you spiritually: Tithe there with joy and gratitude.

If your pastor doesn't feed you spiritually: First, examine your own heart. Are you being fed but resisting the teaching because it challenges you? Are you running from accountability? If you honestly answer no to both questions, and your soul is genuinely starving despite faithful participation—then support the ministry that does feed you while still serving in your local community. But make this decision carefully, with counsel from mature believers who know you well.

If online church feeds you spiritually: That can become your legitimate spiritual storehouse—but only if it includes assembly, accountability, and biblical alignment. Passive content consumption isn't spiritual feeding.

If multiple sources feed you: Give proportionally based on spiritual impact, praying for wisdom about percentages.

If you're changing churches: Be brutally honest about where genuine growth occurs. Are you following the feeding, or are you running from conviction? Seek counsel from people who know you well. If you've changed churches three times in five years, the problem is probably you, not the churches.

What Shandel Discovered

After redirecting her tithe to the ministry consistently feeding her soul, Shandel experienced transformation over two years:

Her spiritual growth accelerated exponentially. The teaching she supported continued challenging her biblical understanding. She found genuine peace about giving instead of guilt-driven obligation. Her relationship with God came alive in unprecedented ways.

"God cares infinitely more about my spiritual growth than my loyalty to buildings," Shandel said. "When I started supporting where I was actually getting fed, my faith became unstoppable."

But Shandel also learned something crucial in the process: she had to honestly examine her reasons for redirecting her tithe. She'd left two churches previously because of offense and conflict. This time was different—she wasn't running from anything. She was running toward the deep teaching her soul desperately needed.

Questions for Your Heart

1. Where do you truly get spiritually fed and grow in faith —and are you honest about whether it's feeding or entertainment?
2. How does knowing Jesus is your eternal High Priest change your tithing approach?
3. What ministry has most impacted your relationship with God—and does it include assembly, accountability, and biblical alignment?
4. Are you leaving your church because God is directing you to deeper feeding, or because you're running from accountability and offense?

A Prayer for Finding Your Spiritual Storehouse

Heavenly Father, thank You for Jesus as my eternal High Priest. Help me see tithing as joyful worship, not religious burden.

Show me clearly where You are feeding me spiritually and helping me grow. Give me wisdom to support ministries that bring Your Word into my life consistently.

But God, also give me the courage to examine my own heart honestly. If I'm running from accountability, convict me. If I'm confusing offense with Your direction, correct me. If I'm chasing entertainment instead of depth, redirect me.

Help me distinguish between Your voice calling me to maturity and my wounded ego directing me away from correction. Give me mature believers who know me well and can tell the truth to me about my patterns.

When my decisions create tension with others, give me grace to follow Your leading while maintaining relationships. Open my heart to give joyfully, knowing my tithe supports Your work in the world.

Make my giving reflect genuine faith in Your provision and gratitude for spiritual transformation. Help me remember that tithing is about relationship and growth, not rules or buildings—and not about my comfort or preference.

In Jesus' name, Amen.

Key Takeaway

Give where you're genuinely spiritually fed and growing in relationship with God. Your tithe should support those who help you understand His Word and develop spiritual maturity—this honors spiritual feeding over institutional loyalty and activates God's blessing on both your giving and your growth. But discerning where God is feeding you requires honest self-examination: Are you following His voice toward depth, or are you running from correction? The difference determines whether you're maturing or merely consuming. Where genuine spiritual feeding occurs—whether local church, online ministry, or multiple sources—it must include assembly, accountability, and biblical alignment, not just passive content consumption.

Chapter 6

The Firstfruits Principle

Stephanie stared at her promotion bonus check—$3,000 she desperately needed. But two words from Sunday's sermon kept echoing in her mind.

The pastor had read from Hebrews:

> "Today, if you hear his voice, do not harden your hearts" (Heb. 3:7-8).

Then from Proverbs:

> "Honor the LORD with your wealth and with the firstfruits of all your produce" (Prov. 3:9 ESV).

The Hebrew word *kavod* means "weight," "honor," or "glory." What you give weight to. What carries importance. What gets honored in your heart.

Stephanie's credit card debt felt heavy. Her daughter's college fund felt heavy. Her mother's medical bills felt heavy. Every financial pressure was screaming for attention, demanding she honor them first.

But God's voice was asking for something different: "Give Me the weight of your allegiance. Honor Me first."

She calculated quickly: The tithe—10% that belonged to God —would be $300. But she felt God prompting beyond that. "Give $500 total—the firstfruits."

The Hebrews passage surfaced again: *Today, if you hear His voice, do not harden your hearts.*

Today. Not tomorrow after she figured out the budget. Not next month after the bills were paid. Today. Right now. With this bonus. She was hearing God's voice about firstfruits.

The question wasn't whether she'd give eventually. The question was whether her heart would stay soft enough to obey what she was hearing today.

Stephanie was about to discover that the weight you give to God in your heart determines whether your heart stays soft and responsive—or hardens like Pharaoh's into self-protective independence.

Two Ways Hearts Become Heavy

The Hebrew word *kavod* means "weight," "honor," or "glory." It describes two opposite realities:

Honoring God:

> "Honor [*kavod*] the LORD with your wealth and with the firstfruits of all your produce; then your barns will be filled with plenty, and your vats will be bursting with wine" (Prov. 3:9-10 ESV).

When you give God weight in your financial decisions—trusting Him with firstfruits before securing yourself—your heart stays soft, responsive, dependent.

Hardening Your Heart:

> "But when Pharaoh saw that there was relief, he hardened [made heavy] his heart and did not listen to them" (see Ex. 8:15).

When you give yourself weight—honoring your security, plans, and fears before trusting God—your heart becomes hard, resistant, independent.

Same word. Opposite directions. The weight in your heart pulls you toward God through trust or away from God through self-reliance.

Centuries after Pharaoh, Hebrews warned:

> "Today, if you hear his voice, do not harden your hearts as in the rebellion, on the day of testing in the wilderness" (Heb. 3:7-8 ESV).

The Hebrew word for wilderness is *midbar*—literally "a place of speaking" or "a place for the word." God led His people into the wilderness specifically to teach them to hear His voice. The wilderness wasn't punishment—it was God's classroom, His speaking-place where He could strip away every competing voice and teach them dependence on His Word alone.

But the wilderness generation, though positioned in God's speaking-place, hardened their hearts through unbelief. They gave more weight to circumstances than to God's voice.

God is still speaking in our wilderness seasons today. When your finances feel barren, when provision seems uncertain, when you're stripped of security—you're in the *midbar*, the place of speaking. The question is: Will you harden your heart toward self-protection, or will you keep it soft by listening to His voice?

Firstfruits giving is the practical test. What gets the weight of your attention when money arrives—God first (soft heart) or your security first (hard heart)?

Every time you receive income, you hear God's voice about firstfruits. Hebrews warns: "Today, if you hear His Voice, do not harden your hearts." Today—with this money, at this moment. Your answer reveals which direction your heart is moving.

Pharaoh's Heavy Heart: When Self-Honor Hardens You

Pharaoh faced ten opportunities to hear God's voice and respond with a soft heart. Ten times, he chose to honor himself instead.

The pattern was consistent: plague → relief → hardening.

> "But when Pharaoh saw that there was relief, he hardened [*kavod* - made heavy] his heart and did not listen to them" (see Ex. 8:15).

Again:

> "But Pharaoh hardened his heart this time also and did not let the people go" (see Ex. 8:32).

Notice the progression: Relief comes → Pharaoh gives weight to his own authority → His heart hardens → He refuses to honor God.

Each time Pharaoh honored himself first, his heart became heavier—harder—more resistant to God's voice. This is exactly what Hebrews warns against: Pharaoh heard God's voice clearly, but "today, if you hear His voice," Pharaoh chose to harden his heart instead.

Pharaoh's hardening reached its climax over firstfruits. God demanded the firstborn of Egypt—the firstfruits of every household. Pharaoh refused to give God what came first. The firstborn belonged to Pharaoh's economy, his workforce, and his future.

The cost of keeping his firstfruits? Losing them entirely.

By the tenth plague, Pharaoh's heart was so hard, so heavy with self-honor, that he couldn't respond even when it cost him his firstborn son.

> "The LORD hardened Pharaoh's heart" (Ex. 10:20)

doesn't mean God forced him—it means God confirmed the direction Pharaoh had chosen. His heart had become immovably heavy toward self-protection.

Pharaoh heard God's voice ten times. Ten times he hardened

his heart. Eventually, his heart became so heavy it couldn't soften anymore.

When God-Honor Keeps You Responsive

While Pharaoh's heart hardened through self-honor, Israel learned the opposite: honoring God first kept their hearts soft and responsive.

> "Set aside a tenth of all that your fields produce each year... so that you may learn to revere [give appropriate weight to] the LORD your God always" (Deut. 14:22-23).

The purpose wasn't funding the temple—it was protecting against hard hearts. When you honor God first, before securing yourself, before knowing how the rest will work out, you're practicing soft-hearted dependence.

This became crucial in the wilderness—the *midbar*, God's speaking-place. God provided manna daily with instructions not to hoard, teaching them to listen for His voice each morning. Some tried keeping extra overnight.

> "It bred worms and stank" (Ex. 16:20 ESV).

When they honored themselves instead of trusting God's voice about daily provision, their hearts began hardening toward self-reliance. They were in the place of speaking, but they weren't listening.

Hebrews references this exact moment:

> "Do not harden your hearts as in the rebellion, on the day of testing in the wilderness" (Heb. 3:8 ESV).

Some kept their hearts soft by trusting Him daily. Others hardened through self-protective hoarding.

The same pattern plays out in our financial wilderness today. When God speaks to you about firstfruits in the *midbar* of your financial uncertainty, you face the same choice Israel faced: Will you hoard what you have in self-protection, or will you honor Him first and trust His voice about provision?

God's promise follows obedience:

> "Honor the LORD with your wealth and with the firstfruits... then your barns will be filled with plenty, and your vats will be bursting with wine" (Prov. 3:9-10 ESV).

Soft hearts that trust God with firstfruits position themselves for provision. Hard hearts that honor themselves first block the very provision they're protecting.

Understanding Firstfruits: The Tithe and Beyond

Firstfruits means giving God priority—setting apart what comes first, not leftovers.

The tithe (10%) is always firstfruits—it comes first because it's holy, set apart for Him. You don't decide whether to return it;

you acknowledge it belongs to Him and honor Him by setting it apart before touching anything else.

But firstfruits can include more than just the tithe. Sometimes God prompts you to give beyond the 10% that's His—an offering from what He's entrusted to you. These offerings are also firstfruits when you give them from the first, not the leftovers.

Both honor God. Both demonstrate soft-hearted trust. But they're different:

- **The tithe (10%)** = Returning His property, acknowledging His ownership
- **Additional offerings** = Generous response to His prompting, given from what He's entrusted to you

When Stephanie felt prompted to give $500 from her $3,000 bonus, she understood: $300 was the tithe that belonged to God. The additional $200 was an offering—a generous response to God's prompting, given from the $2,700 He was entrusting to her care.

Both were firstfruits—given first, before honoring any other demand. Both kept her heart soft. But they honored God in different ways.

Your Pharaoh Moments

Every time money arrives, you face Pharaoh's choice: Honor God first (soft heart) or honor your security first (hardening heart)? The choice seems small. But each time you give weight to self-protection over God-trust, your heart hardens until you can't hear God's voice about finances at all.

Stephanie's Decision

Stephanie sat in her car Sunday afternoon, the $3,000 bonus check in her purse. She'd heard God's voice clearly during prayer: The tithe—$300—belonged to Him. But she felt prompted to give $500 total as firstfruits. The additional $200 would be an offering, a generous response from the $2,700 He'd be entrusting to her.

Her heart wanted to harden. The car payment felt urgent. The credit card balance felt heavy. Her mother's medical bills felt pressing.

But she remembered the Hebrews 3 passage from the morning sermon: "Today, if you hear His Voice, do not harden your hearts."

Today. With this $3,000. Right now.

Stephanie prayed in her car: "God, I'm choosing to honor You first. The $300 belongs to You—that's settled. The additional $200 is an offering—my generous response to Your prompting. I'm giving You the weight of my trust with these firstfruits. My heart wants to harden toward self-protection. But I'm choosing softness through obedience. Help me trust You for what comes next."

She wrote two checks that afternoon—$300 returning the tithe, $200 giving the offering. Her hands shook slightly, but her heart felt soft, responsive, alive to God's voice.

The Following Month

The following month brought unexpected provision: Her boss gave her a $200 monthly raise for additional responsibility. She discovered a car loan error reducing payments by $75 monthly. A forgotten side project paid $400 unexpectedly. Her church gave her $150 in grocery gift cards thanking her for the missions donation.

Total unexpected provision: $825 beyond the $500 she'd given.

"I thought honoring God first would create financial pressure," Stephanie told her small group three months later. "But the opposite happened. Honoring God first with firstfruits—both what belongs to Him and what He prompted as an offering—kept my heart soft. And a soft heart that trusts God positions you for provision in ways a hard heart of self-protection never can.

"Pharaoh's heart hardened because he kept choosing to honor himself when relief came. I chose differently. When my bonus came, I chose to honor God first. My heart stayed soft. And God provided through doors I never imagined."

Stephanie paused. "The real gift wasn't the $825. The real gift was learning I can hear God's voice about money and trust Him enough to obey. That's worth more than any amount He could multiply."

Common Questions About Firstfruits

"What's the difference between tithe and offerings?"

- **Tithe:** 10% that belongs to God. You return it as an acknowledgment of His ownership. It's not yours to decide about—it's already His.
- **Offerings:** Generous response to His prompting (variable, as He leads)

"What If I Can't Afford to Honor God First?"

That's your heart speaking—giving more weight to your circumstances than God's promises. The widow couldn't afford to feed Elijah first. Stephanie couldn't afford to give $500 before her bills.

But they understood: Firstfruits giving isn't about affording—it's about honoring. When you honor God first, you position yourself for His provision. When you honor your security first, you harden your heart toward self-protection.

The question isn't "Can I afford it?" The question is "Will I keep my heart soft by obeying today?"

"What If Nothing Miraculous Happens After I Give?"

Remember—God's faithfulness isn't always immediate financial multiplication. Sometimes He multiplies your money, sometimes your faith, sometimes your character. The question isn't "Will God give me more money?" but "Will I keep my heart soft by honoring Him first?"

"How Do I Know If My Heart Is Hardening?"

Warning signs:

- God's voice about generosity grows quieter
- You rationalize keeping money more than setting it apart
- Financial anxiety dominates despite adequate provision
- You resent when God's voice prompts firstfruits giving
- Other believers' testimonies about provision irritate rather than inspire you

These signs reveal your heart is giving weight to self-protection rather than trusting God.

The remedy? Today, if you hear His voice about firstfruits, do not harden your heart. Choose one act of obedience that honors God first. Let your heart soften through one faithful response.

Your Call to Honor God First

Honoring God with firstfruits means choosing to keep your heart soft when you hear His voice—even when circumstances scream to harden yourself toward self-protection.

This isn't about getting rich. It's about:

- Keeping your heart responsive to God's voice

- Giving Him the weight of your trust
- Resisting the gradual hardening from self-honor
- Positioning yourself for provision through soft-hearted dependence

Every time money arrives, you face two directions:

The Pharaoh direction: Honor yourself first. Give weight to your security. Let your heart harden toward self-protection. Eventually, you can't hear God's voice about finances.

The Voice of the Lord direction: Honor God first. Give weight to His promises. Keep your heart soft through trusting obedience. Stay sensitive to His voice and provision.

Hebrews 3 makes this urgent: "Today, if you hear His Voice, do not harden your hearts."

Not eventually. Not when comfortable. Not after you've secured yourself. Today—right now—with whatever money is in front of you.

The weight of your wealth either draws you closer to God through grateful dependence (soft heart) or pulls you away through self-reliant independence (hard heart).

The firstfruits test reveals which direction you're choosing.

Remember: Your financial wilderness is God's *midbar*—His speaking-place. He's teaching you the same lesson He taught Israel: to listen for His voice and trust His promises even when circumstances scream otherwise. Will you harden your heart like Pharaoh, or will you keep it soft like Israel learned to do?

Questions for Your Heart

1. Today, if you hear God's voice about firstfruits, what is your honest response—trust or resistance?
2. When did you last give God the weight of your allegiance by honoring Him first with money?
3. Looking at your financial decisions over the past month, is your heart moving toward softness (God-honor) or hardness (self-honor)?
4. What "today" decision about firstfruits is God asking you to make right now?

Prayer for Soft Hearts That Honor God

Heavenly Father, I acknowledge that everything comes from You—my health, my abilities, my opportunities, my income. You give me the power to get wealth.

Teach me to honor You with firstfruits, giving You the weight of my trust and allegiance. Help me understand that keeping my heart soft toward Your voice matters more than protecting my security.

Today, if I hear Your voice about generosity, help me not harden my heart like Pharaoh did. When relief comes and I'm tempted to honor myself first, remind me that soft hearts position me for Your provision while hard hearts block Your best.

Help me distinguish between the tithe that belongs to You (which I return as acknowledgment) and offerings You prompt (which I give as generous response). Both are firstfruits when given from the first. Both keep my heart soft. Both honor You.

Give me courage to honor You first even when it feels financially risky. Help me trust that You—who gave me the income in the first place—know exactly how to provide for what I need next.

When anxiety tempts me to give weight to my circumstances instead of Your promises, soften my heart through Your Word. When I start rationalizing self-protection over obedience, speak clearly so I hear Your voice above my fear.

Show me specifically how to honor You with the money You've entrusted to me—not eventually, but today. Help me recognize that each time I choose to honor You first with firstfruits, my heart stays responsive to Your voice. And each time I choose to honor myself first, my heart hardens a little more toward independence.

I don't want Pharaoh's hard heart that couldn't respond to You even at catastrophic cost. I want Israel's soft heart that trusted You daily for manna, that honored You with firstfruits, that stayed responsive to Your voice.

Thank You that my financial wilderness is Your *midbar*—Your speaking-place where You're teaching me to hear Your voice above every competing demand. Help me recognize that You're speaking even when provision seems uncertain, even when circumstances feel barren, even when fear whispers loudest.

Keep my heart soft today, and every day, as long as it is called "today."

In Jesus' name, Amen.

Key Takeaway

The Hebrew word *kavod* (honor/weight/glory) describes both honoring God with firstfruits and hardening your heart through self-protection. The Hebrew word *midbar* (wilderness) literally means "a place of speaking"—God leads you into financial wilderness to teach you to hear His voice and trust His promises when every other security is stripped away. Firstfruits includes both the tithe (10% that belongs to God, returned as acknowledgment) and offerings (generous responses to His prompting, given from what He's entrusted to you)—both honor Him when given from the first, not leftovers. When you give God the weight of your allegiance by honoring Him first with your wealth, your heart stays soft and responsive to His voice—positioned for provision that exceeds your calculations. When you honor your own security first, your heart gradually hardens like Pharaoh's—each choice to keep firstfruits for yourself makes you heavier toward self-reliance and more resistant to God's voice. Hebrews 3 makes this urgent: "Today, if you hear His voice, do not harden your hearts." Firstfruits giving isn't just about money—it's the practical test that reveals who truly gets the weight of honor in your heart today, and whether your heart is moving toward soft responsiveness or hard independence in God's speaking-place.

Chapter 7

Complete Surrender and Devoted Things

What if God asked you to give away the one thing you've prayed for desperately? Not donate generously from surplus, but surrender completely what you value most—never to hold it again?

Most of us are willing to give God something. A percentage. A portion. A generous gift. But what happens when God asks for everything? When He wants complete surrender of the very thing your heart treasures most?

This isn't theoretical. Throughout Scripture, God has asked His people to give Him things completely—not partially, not eventually, but entirely and immediately. The Hebrew word for this is *cherem*—devoted things that belong wholly to God.

When God says something is *cherem*, there's no room for negotiation. No space for partial obedience. No option to keep the "best parts" for yourself. Devoted things belong entirely to Him.

The question is: When God asks for something completely, will you hear His voice and obey?

When God Asked for Everything at Jericho

When Joshua led Israel into the Promised Land, their first military target was Jericho. God gave specific instructions about the city's wealth:

> "The city and all that is in it are to be devoted to the LORD" (Josh. 6:17).

Everything in Jericho was *cherem*—completely devoted to God. The silver, the gold, the valuable articles—all of it belonged to the LORD's treasury. Not a single Israelite could keep anything for personal use.

This wasn't about destroying property for destruction's sake. God was teaching His people something foundational: Nothing—not even the spoils of their first victory in the Promised Land—could rival their devotion to Him. Their treasure belonged to Him completely.

The command was clear. The expectation was absolute. Obedience was not optional.

But one man decided he knew better.

Achan's Fatal Mistake

Achan saw a beautiful robe from Babylonia, two hundred shekels of silver, and a bar of gold weighing fifty shekels. And he wanted them.

> "When I saw in the plunder a beautiful robe from Babylonia, two hundred shekels of silver and

> a bar of gold weighing fifty shekels, I coveted them and took them. They are hidden in the ground inside my tent, with the silver underneath" (Josh. 7:21).

Four verbs that destroyed everything: saw, coveted, took, hid.

Achan kept what God said belonged entirely to Him. He reasoned that surely God wouldn't miss a few items from Jericho's vast wealth. He calculated that his small disobedience wouldn't matter in the grand scheme of Israel's conquest.

He was catastrophically wrong.

Israel's next battle—against the tiny city of Ai—ended in humiliating defeat. Thirty-six Israelite soldiers died. The entire nation's morale collapsed. Joshua fell facedown before God, crying out for answers.

God's response was direct:

> "Israel has sinned; they have violated my covenant, which I commanded them to keep. They have taken some of the devoted things; they have stolen, they have lied, they have put them with their own possessions" (Josh. 7:11).

One man's decision to keep what God wanted completely brought disaster on an entire nation. Achan, his family, and everything he owned were destroyed.

The cost of keeping what God asked for completely was total loss. Achan's tragedy teaches us that devoted things aren't ours to negotiate about. When God says something belongs entirely to Him, partial obedience is complete disobedience.

Hannah's Impossible Vow

But devoted things aren't always about destruction. Sometimes God asks us to give Him completely what we treasure most—not to destroy it, but to surrender it entirely for His purposes.

Hannah's story shows us what this looks like when obedience costs everything.

Hannah was barren. In ancient Israel, childlessness wasn't just personal grief—it was social shame. Year after year, her husband's other wife Peninnah had children while Hannah's arms remained empty. Peninnah mocked her constantly.

The annual trip to Shiloh for worship became an annual humiliation. One year, her grief became unbearable.

> "In her deep anguish Hannah prayed to the LORD, weeping bitterly" (1 Sam. 1:10).

Eli the priest, watching her lips move without sound, thought she was drunk. That's how intense her grief appeared.

But Hannah wasn't drunk. She was making a vow that would change Israel's history.

> "LORD Almighty, if you will only look on your servant's misery and remember me, and not

> forget your servant but give her a son, then I will give him to the LORD for all the days of his life, and no razor will ever be used on his head" (1 Sam. 1:11).

She was asking God for a son—the one thing she wanted most desperately—and simultaneously promising to give him back completely. Not "I'll dedicate him to Your service." Not "when he's older." "I will give him to the LORD for all the days of his life."

Hannah made her unborn son a devoted thing before he was even conceived. And something remarkable happened. After making that vow,

> "her face was no longer downcast" (1 Sam. 1:18).

Peace came before the answer. She heard God's voice through her own vow. And peace came through complete surrender.

The Waiting and The Surrender

God remembered Hannah. She conceived and gave birth to Samuel. But the vow still stood.

> "After he was weaned, she took the boy with her, young as he was" (1 Sam. 1:24).

Weaning typically happened when a child was three to five years old. Hannah had years of nursing Samuel, raising him, loving him—all while knowing she would have to give him away.

Every morning when Samuel woke up. Every milestone—first words, first steps, first prayers—shadowed by the knowledge that she'd made him a devoted thing. Did she ever try to negotiate? "Maybe I could keep him until he's seven. Maybe he could visit often."

The text doesn't tell us about those internal struggles. But we know she was human. We know she loved her son desperately.

The day came. Samuel was weaned. Hannah brought him to Shiloh, to Eli the priest. Can you imagine that journey? Leading her young son by the hand, knowing she'd return without him?

She found Eli:

> "Pardon me, my lord. As surely as you live, I am the woman who stood here beside you praying to the LORD. I prayed for this child, and the LORD has granted me what I asked of him. So now I give him to the LORD. For his whole life he will be given over to the LORD" (1 Sam. 1:26-28).

Past tense. "I give him." The surrender was complete. Not "I'll visit often" or "until he's older." For his whole life.

And then—remarkably—

> "And he worshiped the LORD there" (1 Sam. 1:28).

After giving away her son, Hannah worshiped.

Her prayer in 1 Samuel 2:1-2 isn't grief. It's praise:

> "My heart rejoices in the LORD; in the LORD my horn is lifted high... There is no one holy like the LORD; there is no one besides you; there is no Rock like our God."

She worshiped after surrendering what she treasured most. Because she'd heard God's voice through her vow, obeyed despite the cost, and discovered that He's more valuable than anything she was holding onto.

Understanding Vows and Devoted Things

Hannah's vow reveals something crucial about devoted things: Not everything devoted to God is commanded by Him. Sometimes we voluntarily make things devoted through our own vows.

The difference matters.

Cherem - God declares something devoted to Him (like Jericho's wealth, the Amalekites). This is irrevocable from the moment God speaks it. No negotiation. No redemption. Complete surrender is required.

Neder (vow) - You voluntarily dedicate something to the Lord. Once spoken, your vow becomes binding like *cherem*. What was optional before the vow becomes obligatory afterwards.

Hannah wasn't commanded by God to give Samuel away. She chose to make that vow. But the moment she spoke those words—"I will give him to the LORD for all the days of his life"—Samuel became a devoted thing. Her voluntary dedication took on the irrevocable nature of *cherem*.

That's why Scripture treats vows with such seriousness:

> "When you vow a vow to God, do not delay paying it, for he has no pleasure in fools. Pay what you vow. It is better that you should not vow than that you should vow and not pay" (Eccl. 5:4-5 ESV).

Better not to vow at all than to vow and fail to honor it.

The principle extends to the New Testament. Ananias and Sapphira sold property and vowed to give the proceeds to the church. But they kept back part of the price while claiming to give everything.

Peter's rebuke cut to the heart of the issue:

> "While it remained unsold, did it not remain your own? And after it was sold, was it not at your disposal? Why is it that you have contrived this deed in your heart? You have not lied to man but to God" (Acts 5:4 ESV).

Before their vow, the property was theirs. After they vowed to give it, keeping any part was lying to God. Their voluntary dedication became binding the moment they spoke it.

Both died immediately.

God takes vows seriously because vows reveal what we truly believe about His authority. When you make something devoted through your vow, you're placing it under the dominion of God's kingdom. It takes on the characteristics of *cherem*—irrevocable, non-negotiable, completely His.

Hannah understood this. She could have avoided the vow entirely—God might have given her a son anyway. But once she spoke those words in the temple, Samuel belonged to the LORD. Years of raising him, loving him, treasuring him didn't change what her vow had established.

When the time came to fulfill her vow, partial obedience wasn't an option. "Maybe I'll keep him until he's older" would have been breaking covenant with God. The devoted thing had to be surrendered completely.

Whether God declares something *cherem* or you voluntarily make it devoted through a vow, the principle remains: devoted things belong entirely to Him. Your obedience reveals whether you truly trust His heart more than you trust your treasure.

The Multiplication

The story doesn't end with Hannah's empty arms.

> "And the LORD was gracious to Hannah; she gave birth to three sons and two daughters" (1 Sam. 2:21).

She gave God one son. He gave her five more children.

But the multiplication extended far beyond Hannah's household. Samuel became one of Israel's greatest prophets. The child she devoted to God became God's voice to an entire nation. He anointed kings. Israel's entire monarchy flowed through the boy Hannah gave completely to the LORD.

And young Samuel became famous for hearing God's voice. In 1 Samuel 3, the boy sleeping in the temple heard the LORD calling his name. Samuel became the prophet who taught a generation to hear God's voice—because his mother had heard God's voice through her vow and obeyed completely.

Hannah's devoted thing shaped Israel's history for generations. She simply heard God's voice, lived with it for years, and finally obeyed completely when the time came.

Her complete surrender of what she loved most became God's instrument for blessing a nation.

Mae's Jewelry Box

Mae sat in her living room; the wooden jewelry box lay open in front of her. Each piece held a memory she couldn't bear to lose.

Her husband Robert had died two years earlier after thirty-four years of marriage. The jewelry he'd given her over those decades was her connection to the life they'd built together. The anniversary necklace. The birthday earrings. The sapphire pendant from their Hawaii trip. The diamond bracelet—his last gift before the cancer diagnosis.

Each piece held a moment. A memory. A fragment of the man she'd lost.

Mae had attended a missions conference at her church the previous Sunday. A missionary shared about a ministry training women in Southeast Asia—many rescued from trafficking, learning vocational skills to support their families and rebuild their lives.

The ministry was $15,000 short of their annual budget. Without it, eight women currently in the program would have to drop out.

During prayer after the service, Mae couldn't shake a thought that felt like God's voice: "Your jewelry."

"That's insane," she whispered. "Those are my memories. My children expect to inherit them."

But the thought persisted. "Your jewelry could change their future."

Mae drove home in silence. By the time she pulled into her driveway, she knew what she needed to do. She just didn't know if she had the courage.

The Family Meeting

Mae called her children—her daughter Lisa and her son David—and asked them to come over Saturday. When they arrived, concern written on their faces, Mae pulled out the jewelry box.

"I want to talk to you about Dad's jewelry," Mae said. "I'm thinking about selling all of it and giving the money to a missions organization."

The room went silent.

David spoke first, measured but opposed. "Mom, Dad worked hard to buy you those pieces. Doesn't selling them dishonor his memory?"

Lisa was less diplomatic. "Are you serious? Those are family heirlooms!"

The conversation grew tense. Lisa left without hugging her goodbye. David kissed her cheek but looked disappointed.

Maybe they were right. Maybe giving everything was excessive. Maybe God would be satisfied with partial obedience.

Three Weeks of Wrestling

Mae spent three weeks wrestling with God's prompting and her children's resistance.

Daily, she'd hold each piece, remembering. The emerald earrings from David's birth. The sapphire pendant from their Hawaii anniversary. The diamond bracelet—Robert's last gift before his diagnosis.

"God, are You really asking for all of it?" she prayed. "Can't I keep just one piece?"

Week three, her Bible reading brought her to Hannah's story. These words caught her attention:

> "I prayed for this child, and the LORD has granted me what I asked of him. So now I give him to the LORD. For his whole life he will be given over to the LORD" (1 Sam. 1:27-28).

Hannah gave what she'd prayed for desperately. Not partially, not temporarily, but completely.

Mae heard God's voice through Hannah's example: "I'm not asking you to forget Robert. I'm asking you to trust Me completely."

The jewelry was beautiful. The memories were precious. But they weren't more precious than obedience.

That afternoon, Mae made an appointment with an estate jewelry appraiser.

The Appraisal and Decision

Mae had assumed the collection might be worth eight to ten thousand dollars. The appraiser examined each piece carefully for an hour, then looked up.

"Mrs. Thomas, some of these pieces have appreciated significantly. Based on current market values, I'd estimate the entire collection at eighteen thousand five hundred dollars."

More than enough to fund the training program. More than enough to help all eight women complete their education.

Mae drove home in a daze and sat in her driveway with her hands on the steering wheel. "Okay, God," she said aloud to her empty car. "I hear You. I'm doing this."

Her hands were shaking, but her decision was firm.

Nine Months of Silence

Mae sold the jewelry and sent the full $18,500 to the missions organization, with a note: "For the women in your training program. In memory of my husband Robert, who taught me that generosity honors God."

Her children's reactions were painful. "I can't believe you did that," Lisa said, voice cold. David was quieter but hurt: "I hope you know what you're doing."

Lisa stopped calling. David's calls grew brief and strained.

Weeks became months. No dramatic provision appeared. Her modest retirement income continued. Bills stayed the same. Nothing visible changed.

Friends looked uncomfortable when she mentioned the jewelry. Most changed the subject.

By month six, Mae questioned herself. Had she heard God correctly? Or had she made a terrible mistake?

Month seven brought crisis. Her car needed $1,200 in repairs she could barely afford. "I could have paid this with the jewelry money," she thought, signing the check.

The enemy's whisper came loud that night: "You gave away your husband's memory for nothing."

Mae lay awake wondering if she'd been foolish instead of faithful.

The Letter

Nine months later, a thick envelope arrived. Inside: photos of eight women at sewing machines, holding up finished garments and graduation certificates.

The letter explained that Mae's gift had funded their final semester. All eight had graduated, found employment, and were now supporting families.

One woman's translated note was included:

"My name is Sophea. For three years, I was told I was worthless. Your gift paid for my last four months of training. I wanted to quit many times, but teachers said someone in America believed in me. I couldn't let that person down.

I graduated three weeks ago. I have a job now. My children can eat every day. They go to school. They are safe.

I don't know who you are. But I pray for you every morning. Thank you for hearing God and obeying. You changed my life."

Mae read the letter three times, tears streaming.

She drove to Lisa's house that afternoon, the letter and photos in hand. They hadn't spoken for two months.

Lisa read slowly, her expression changing to tears. "Mom, I'm sorry. I didn't understand. You weren't throwing away Dad's memory—you were honoring his generous heart. He would have loved this."

They cried together over photos of women they'd never meet but whose lives were forever changed.

David called that evening after Lisa sent him photos. "Mom, I've been wrong. You heard God more clearly than any of us. I'm proud of you."

Two Years Later

Mae doesn't regret selling the jewelry. When people ask if she misses it, she's honest: "Sometimes. Especially on my anniversary, or Robert's birthday."

But then she pulls out the photos from Southeast Asia. Eight women, smiling, holding graduation certificates. Eight women supporting families. Eight women building futures.

"I didn't give the jewelry to get my family back or receive a thank-you letter," Mae says. "I gave it because God asked for it completely, and I'd learned from Hannah that devoted things aren't mine to negotiate about.

"But God is faithful. He gave me peace, reconciliation with my children, and the joy of knowing eight women's lives were changed. Some treasures can't be worn around your neck—they're written in heaven."

Last Christmas, Lisa gave her mother a framed photo of the eight women with Sophea's letter matted beside it. "This is your real inheritance, Mom," Lisa said. "Not jewelry. This. Lives changed because you heard God and obeyed."

Mae keeps it on her mantle, next to Robert's photo. Every morning when she sees it, she remembers that devoted things belong completely to God. And His faithfulness after surrender exceeds anything we're holding onto.

What This Means for You

Some things God asks for completely, not partially.

These might be possessions, like Hannah's son or Mae's jewelry. They might be dreams—the career path you've planned, the relationship you're clinging to, the future you've mapped out. They might be comfort, control, or security.

When God asks for something entirely, partial obedience is total disobedience.

Achan kept part of what God wanted completely, and it cost him everything. But Hannah surrendered completely what she treasured most, and her obedience shaped a nation. Mae gave away jewelry that held precious memories, and women's lives were transformed.

The difference wasn't the thing surrendered. The difference was complete obedience versus partial negotiation.

How to Recognize Devoted Things

You can't stop thinking about it during prayer. Scripture arrests your attention about surrender, like it did for Mae when she read Hannah's story. Peace comes when you decide to give; anxiety comes when you decide to keep. Trusted counsel confirms what you're sensing. And often, the cost feels impossibly high—which is frequently the confirmation that this is what God wants.

Devoted things test whether you'll hear God's voice and trust Him enough to surrender what you treasure most.

God doesn't always multiply devoted things materially. Hannah received five more children, but that wasn't guaranteed when she surrendered Samuel. Mae experienced family reconciliation and impact in Southeast Asia, but she had nine months of silence and doubt first.

Some rewards are immediate. Some come slowly. Some are eternal and won't be fully seen until heaven.

But God's faithfulness never fails. When you surrender completely what He asks for, you discover—like Hannah, like

Mae—that He's more valuable than anything you're holding onto.

The Question Only You Can Answer

What is God asking you to give Him completely?

You know what it is. That thing you keep negotiating about in prayer. That possession or dream or relationship you keep trying to bargain over. That devoted thing you're tempted to keep "just this part" while surrendering the rest.

Hannah could have kept Samuel home, reasoning that God wouldn't really want her to give up her child. Mae could have sold half the jewelry and kept her favorites.

But both understood that devoted things belong completely to God. Partial obedience would have been total disobedience.

God isn't asking for devoted things because He's cruel. He's asking because He wants your whole heart—and He knows your treasure reveals where your heart truly resides.

When you surrender completely what you love most, you discover what Hannah and Mae discovered: He's more valuable than anything you're holding onto. His plans for your devoted thing exceed anything you could plan. His faithfulness after surrender surpasses your greatest treasure.

Hannah worshiped after giving Samuel away. Not because it didn't hurt. Not because it was easy. But because she'd heard God's voice, obeyed completely, and discovered that God Himself is the treasure that satisfies.

The devoted thing God is asking you to surrender completely —will you hear His voice and obey?

Your answer to that question will shape everything that follows.

Questions for Your Heart

1. What is God asking you to surrender completely that you've been trying to give partially?
2. What would it cost you to make your most treasured possession a "devoted thing" for God alone?
3. How has holding onto what God asked for completely affected your relationship with Him?
4. What does Hannah's worship after surrendering Samuel teach you about trusting God with devoted things?

Prayer

Heavenly Father, You know the thing You're asking me to surrender completely. It's the treasure I've been holding back, the devoted thing I've been negotiating about. You know why it's hard—why I've rationalized keeping it, why I've tried partial obedience.

Give me Hannah's courage to make a vow and keep it, even when the cost is everything I treasure. Give me Mae's faith to surrender what holds memories and meaning. Help me hear Your voice clearly when You ask for something completely.

I don't want to be like Achan, hiding what belongs to You. I want to be like Hannah—able to worship after surrendering what I love most, because I trust Your heart more than I trust my treasure.

Show me what You want completely. Give me courage to obey. And help me trust that Your faithfulness after surrender exceeds anything I'm holding onto.

In Jesus' name, Amen.

Key Takeaway

When God asks for something completely, partial obedience is total disobedience. Hannah surrendered her son Samuel entirely to the LORD for all the days of his life, and he became God's voice to a nation. Mae gave away jewelry holding precious memories, and eight women's futures were transformed. Devoted things aren't ours to negotiate about—they're tests of whether we'll hear God's voice and trust Him enough to surrender what we treasure most, discovering that His faithfulness after complete surrender exceeds anything we're holding onto and that He Himself is the treasure that truly satisfies.

Chapter 8
Distinguishing God's Voice

Brenda faced two job offers that would determine her future. One paid twice as much but required moving across the country away from family. The other paid significantly less but brought immediate peace to her heart.

"God, which one should I choose?" Brenda prayed.

She'd heard about "obeying God's voice" in sermons, but how do you actually hear it? And how do you know it's really Him speaking?

Brenda chose the lower-paying position based on the supernatural peace flooding her heart whenever she considered it. Within six months, she received two promotions, met her future husband at the company, and found work that utilized her gifts perfectly.

"God's voice brought peace that led to blessings beyond my imagination," Brenda said. "His way proved infinitely better than what seemed logical."

What Happens When You Obey God's Voice

In a world full of financial pressures and competing voices, the real question isn't how to accumulate more wealth but how to align your life completely with God's desires.

The blessings God promises flow naturally from hearts completely committed to obeying His voice in all circumstances.

> "If you fully obey the LORD your God and carefully follow all his commands I give you today, the LORD your God will set you high above all the nations on earth. All these blessings will come on you and accompany you if you obey the LORD your God" (Deut. 28:1-2).

Blessings aren't the goal—they're the byproduct of lives completely surrendered to following God's guidance consistently.

Samuel emphasized this truth to King Saul:

> "Does the LORD delight in burnt offerings and sacrifices as much as in obeying the LORD? To obey is better than sacrifice, and to heed is better than the fat of rams. For rebellion is like the sin of divination, and arrogance like the evil of idolatry" (1 Sam. 15:22-23).

Obedience unlocks God's supernatural provision in ways that religious activity alone cannot accomplish.

How to Actually Hear God's Voice

The Hebrew word for "obey" means hearing and then acting

decisively on what you heard. Faithful obedience begins with listening carefully and responding with immediate action.

Common Ways God Speaks Today:

Through Peace in Your Heart: A deep sense of rightness about specific decisions, supernatural calmness even when choices seem risky, inner peace that doesn't depend on favorable circumstances.

Through Open and Closed Doors: Opportunities that arrive unexpectedly at perfect timing, obstacles that prevent certain paths you were considering, circumstances that align perfectly despite your planning.

Through Wise Counsel: Godly people giving similar advice independently, mentors who speak biblical truth into your life, friends who confirm what you're already sensing.

Through Scripture: Bible verses that speak directly to your situation, passages that won't leave your mind or heart, truth that applies specifically to your current decision.

Through Persistent Thoughts: Ideas that won't disappear despite your resistance, thoughts that align with biblical truth and God's character, impressions that grow stronger with prayer.

Here's what makes recognition possible: a willing heart hears differently than a reluctant one. When your heart is closed—defensive, already decided, building arguments—God's voice sounds like an unreasonable demand. But when your heart is willing—open, receptive, genuinely seeking His direction—His voice sounds like the invitation it is. You can't hear clearly what you're unwilling to obey.

My Own Journey: When God Asked Me to Leave Successful Ministry

It was in 2003. I'd been in ministry for seven years, pouring my life into building something I believed God had called me to create.

Our ministry classroom was packed that morning—people whose lives had been transformed by God's Word, new faces walking in every week, a community that had grown beyond what I'd imagined when we started.

I stood at the back of the classroom, watching people worship, seeing the connections forming, feeling the presence of God in that space.

That's when I heard the question clearly in my spirit: *Do you think you can give all of this up?*

I froze.

My immediate internal response was confusion. "I don't understand. Isn't this what a successful ministry should look like? People are being transformed. The room is full. More people keep coming."

Then came the harder questions from my own heart: "Why should I leave this? How does walking away from fruitful ministry make any sense?"

But underneath the confusion was something deeper—a sense that ministry success had become part of my identity, my purpose, perhaps even my security. I'd built something, and I was proud of it. The thought of walking away felt like I was losing part of myself.

Yet even in that moment of shock and resistance, I knew I'd heard God's voice. It had that unmistakable quality—peaceful but disruptive, clear but challenging, loving but demanding.

I looked over at my wife across the room. She was engaged in conversation, completely unaware of the internal earthquake I was experiencing.

I made a decision right then: "Lord, I'm willing to let this go. But You're going to have to speak to my wife directly. I won't mention this to her. She needs to hear from You, not from me."

The Waiting Period

Days turned into weeks. Weeks turned into months.

I kept leading ministry. I kept teaching. But something had shifted inside me. I was holding everything loosely, waiting for confirmation that I hadn't misheard God's voice.

About a year after that evening in the classroom, my wife was driving alone in her car. She wasn't thinking about ministry or big life decisions. She was just driving.

Then she heard God speak to her spirit clearly: *You should listen to your husband. I do speak to him.*

When she told me what she'd heard, I felt a surge of excitement mixed with holy fear. God had confirmed His word through my wife without me saying anything. He spoke to both of us independently about the same direction.

The Decision

We sat down together and talked about what stepping away would actually look like.

We approached our pastor and explained what we'd been hearing from God. "We believe the Lord is releasing us to the next phase of our ministry journey," I said. The words felt both right and challenging.

The pastor was gracious. He blessed us. But I could see the questions in his eyes—the same questions I'd been wrestling with for months: Why leave something that's working?

The Wilderness Season

For six months, we were in what felt like wilderness.

We enrolled in a school of ministry to grow and develop new skills. We moved to a new location, starting over in many ways. I began developing in a school of the prophetic—learning to hear God's voice even more clearly, ironically.

But it felt like the wilderness. The sense of purpose and impact I'd known in the classroom was gone. I wasn't reaching "many people" anymore. I wasn't seeing the weekly transformations.

I questioned daily whether I'd made the right choice. Had I really heard from God? Or had I walked away from something fruitful for no good reason?

During those six months, I learned something crucial: obedience to God's voice often requires walking through seasons where nothing makes sense by human logic. The fruit isn't always immediate. Clarity doesn't always come quickly.

But God was faithful through the confusion.

The Fruit—Years Later

Now, years after that decision, I can see what God was doing.

First outcome: All the things the Lord had been teaching us over many years—through the ministry classroom, through wilderness, through the school of the prophetic—came together like pieces of a puzzle. We'd been equipped in ways we couldn't have been if we'd stayed in that comfortable, successful ministry.

Second outcome: We learned to minister God's love to more people and in a greater way than we'd been able to before. Not just reaching people in one classroom, but impacting lives across different contexts, different communities, different expressions of ministry.

Third outcome: I learned what it meant to hear God's voice about finances and obedience. That decision to leave successful ministry—and trust God through the wilderness season that followed—became the foundation for everything in this book. You can't teach people to hear God's voice about their wallet if you haven't learned to hear His voice about your whole life.

Looking back now, I understand what God was asking that morning in 2003. He wasn't asking me to leave ministry. He was asking me to leave my attachment to ministry success as my identity and security.

He wanted me to learn that following His voice matters more than visible results.

He wanted me to experience that His provision comes through obedience, not through clinging to what seems safe.

He wanted me to discover that wilderness seasons aren't punishment—they're preparation.

The ministry I thought I was giving up? It was nothing compared to what God had prepared for the years ahead. But I never would have experienced it if I'd said, "I can't leave this success behind."

Isaac's Supernatural Harvest During Famine

Isaac's life provides a powerful biblical example of blessings that follow obedience to God's voice.

During severe famine, God told Isaac not to go to Egypt for food but to stay in the land He would show him, despite obvious scarcity and difficulty.

Everyone else was fleeing to Egypt. Logic screamed: "Go where there's food!"

But Isaac heard God's voice clearly: *Stay.*

Isaac obeyed God's direction and planted crops during the famine—an act that seemed insane to anyone watching. You don't plant during famine. You flee to where there's already food.

He reaped a hundredfold harvest that same year: "

> Isaac planted crops in that land, and the same

> year reaped a hundredfold, because the LORD blessed him. The man became rich, and his wealth continued to grow until he became very wealthy. He had so many flocks and herds and servants that the Philistines envied him" (Gen. 26:12-14).

Isaac's story demonstrates that obedience to God's voice leads to extraordinary blessings even during challenging circumstances when logical decisions would point elsewhere.

Voices That Compete with God's Voice

Today we face a spiritual famine—a famine of hearing, honoring, and trusting God's voice above other influences.

> "'The days are coming,' declares the Sovereign LORD, 'when I will send a famine through the land—not a famine of food or a thirst for water, but a famine of hearing the words of the LORD'" (Amos 8:11).

The Voice of Fear: "What if this doesn't work out as planned? You can't afford to take that financial risk. Play it safe and choose the secure option."

The Voice of Pride: "You deserve better than this opportunity. Don't let people think you're weak or foolish. You've worked too hard to give this up now."

The Voice of Greed: "Take the money while you can get it. Think about your long-term financial security. You need more wealth to be truly happy."

The Voice of People-Pleasing: "What will others think about your choice? Don't disappoint your family's expectations. Everyone expects you to choose this path."

The Voice of Comparison: "Look at what everyone else has. You're falling behind financially. You need to catch up with your peers."

These competing voices are loud, persistent, and often sound reasonable. Learning to distinguish God's voice from these counterfeits is one of the most critical skills for faithful financial stewardship.

How to Practice Hearing God's Voice

Step 1: Create Space for Listening

Remove distractions that compete for your attention. Ask God to speak and then wait patiently. Write down the thoughts and impressions you receive.

Step 2: Test What You Hear

Does it align with Scripture and God's character? Does it bring peace or create anxiety and fear? Do wise, mature counselors confirm what you're sensing? Does it point toward love, service, and God's kingdom?

Step 3: Start with Small Things

Practice listening to God in daily, low-stakes decisions. Obey consistently in little things to build confidence. Look for His guidance in routine choices.

Step 4: Act on What You Hear

Take the first step even if you can't see the complete path. Obey quickly when you sense His clear direction. Don't wait for more confirmation if you already know what He's saying.

Step 5: Learn from the Results

Notice how peace follows obedience to His voice. See how God provides when you trust Him completely. Observe how His way proves better than your own planning.

Common Questions About Hearing God

"How do I know if it's really God's voice?"

God's voice will always agree with biblical truth, bring peace rather than confusion, point toward love and service, be confirmed by wise counselors, and lead to spiritual growth.

"What if I'm wrong about what I heard?"

Start with smaller decisions to build confidence. God is patient with sincere seekers. He'd rather you try to obey and make mistakes than not try at all because of fear.

"What if obeying God doesn't make financial sense?"

Remember Isaac, who farmed during famine and reaped a hundredfold harvest. God's mathematics are different from the world's calculations. His provision follows obedience, not the other way around.

Questions for Your Heart

1. When did you last choose obedience over what seemed easier or more profitable?
2. How do you usually sense God's guidance in your life?
3. Which competing voices do you struggle with most in your decision-making?
4. What is God saying to you right now that you've been hesitant to obey?

Prayer for Hearing and Obeying God

Lord, help me tune my heart consistently to Your voice and listen carefully for Your guidance. Let my focus be on Your will rather than money, possessions, or worldly success.

Teach me to trust completely in Your provision and seek first Your kingdom in all things. Guide me through every challenge and decision with Your perfect wisdom.

Give me courage to obey even when it doesn't make sense to others or seems risky according to worldly standards. Help me recognize Your voice clearly among all the competing voices in my life.

When obedience leads to difficulty or uncertainty, strengthen my faith to trust Your character over my circumstances. Show me specific areas where I need to trust You more and rely on my own understanding less.

Thank You for being faithful even when I'm confused. Thank You for providing even when the path through wilderness is unclear. Thank You for speaking even when I'm slow to hear.

May my life demonstrate Your love, wisdom, and faithfulness through consistent obedience. Help me remember that Your way is always better than my way.

In Jesus' name, Amen.

Key Takeaway

God's voice brings peace, guidance, and blessing to those who listen carefully and obey faithfully. When you choose obedience over convenience consistently—even through wilderness seasons where nothing makes sense—you position yourself for God's best, which is always better than what you could achieve on your own through human wisdom and planning alone. A willing heart hears God's voice as invitation; a reluctant heart hears it as unreasonable demand. The difference between the two determines whether you experience the extraordinary provision that follows obedience or miss what God has prepared because you couldn't let go of what seemed safe.

Part I Summary

The Voice You've Learned to Recognize

You began Part One with a fundamental question: **Whose voice controls your wallet?**

Through these chapters, you've discovered that every financial decision is ultimately a choice about which voice you will obey —not which advice sounds smartest, but which voice you trust most deeply.

What You've Learned About Heaven

Along the way, you've established three foundational realities that change everything.

Your Royal Identity

You are not a desperate beggar negotiating with God for survival. You are a child of the King—entrusted with His resources and invited into partnership with His purposes. This identity reshapes how you view every dollar you manage.

Worship Through Finances

Generosity is not an obligation to fulfill; it is worship. When you give your firstfruits, you are declaring with your wallet what you proclaim with your words: *"God, You are my source, my provider, my Lord."*

Learning Whose Voice to Follow

You have learned to recognize the voices competing for control of your finances. Fear's voice sounds urgent and protective. Culture's voice sounds reasonable and safe. But God's voice—though it sometimes asks the impossible—leads to provision, peace, and purpose that fear's whisper can never deliver.

A Shift of the Heart

Something has changed within you.

You no longer see your wallet as something to protect, but as something to steward.
You no longer view giving as loss, but as worship.
You are beginning to trust that God's voice—even when it asks you to open your hand—leads somewhere better than fear ever could.

Your heart is being positioned.
Your identity is being established.
You are learning whose voice to follow.

The Bridge to House

Heaven has taught you to recognize God's voice.

House will teach you what that voice promises about provision for *your* household.

When bills exceed income, what does He promise?
When anxiety steals sleep, what does He whisper?

Let's discover what happens when God speaks—specifically and personally—about your household's needs.

Part II

House

Hearing God Promise Provision for YOU

Katrina stared at the eviction notice taped to her apartment door. Thirty days. She had thirty days to come up with three months' back rent—$4,200—or she and her two kids would be homeless.

Her bank account showed $847. Her next paycheck would barely cover groceries and utilities.

The math was impossible.

She sat on her couch that night, the notice trembling in her hands, and heard the familiar voices competing for control. *Apply for credit cards. Borrow from your parents. Stop tithing until you're caught up. God will understand.*

But during her morning quiet time three weeks earlier, a single phrase from Matthew 6 had captured her attention: "Your heavenly Father knows that YOU need all these things."

Not "God provides generally." Not "God cares for people in the abstract."

Your heavenly Father knows that YOU need all these things.

Katrina closed her eyes. "God, do You see MY crisis? Do You have a plan for MY rent and MY kids?"

The peace that came wasn't a dollar amount. It wasn't a clear solution. It was the quiet assurance that He saw HER specific situation—and He cared.

From Worship to Provision

Part I taught you to recognize God's voice calling you to worship Him with your finances. You learned to distinguish His voice from fear's whisper, to respond with willing devotion rather than reluctant obligation.

Now comes the next question: What does God's voice promise about provision for YOUR household?

Jesus made it clear:

> "Your heavenly Father knows that YOU need them all" (Matt. 6:32).

He's not distant from YOUR circumstances. He sees YOUR empty account, YOUR midnight panic, YOUR bills due tomorrow.

And He's speaking—making promises about provision for YOUR specific needs.

The Question Part II Answers

Will you trust what God says about YOUR household even when YOUR math doesn't work?

The chapters ahead show people who heard God's promises about provision for THEIR crises, chose to believe despite impossible circumstances, and experienced His faithfulness in ways they couldn't imagine.

YOUR crisis is waiting. So is His promise.

Chapter 9

When YOUR Math Fails

Prayer That Moves Heaven

Renee spread the bills across her bed for the third time that week. No matter how she calculated, the numbers told the same story: $1,847 in immediate obligations, $1,203 in available funds.

Her hands trembled as she sorted out the stack—electric company's final notice, car payment overdue; grocery money already spent on prescription medication. Her eight-year-old son asked why she looked worried.

How do you explain mathematical impossibility to a child? More importantly, how do you pray when the math doesn't work?

Renee was about to discover that impossible circumstances create perfect conditions for hearing God's voice about YOUR specific needs.

When Starvation Becomes Imminent

The widow of Zarephath faced certain death during devastating famine. She possessed exactly enough flour and oil for one final meal.

Staring at her nearly empty jars, she made a heartbreaking decision:

> "I'll prepare this last food for my son and myself. Then we'll wait to die" (see 1 Kings 17:12).

This wasn't pessimism—she was genuinely out of options. Then Elijah appeared, requesting water and bread.

Her response revealed total desperation:

> "I don't have any bread—only a handful of flour in a jar and a little olive oil in a jug. I am gathering a few sticks to take home and make a meal for myself and my son, that we may eat it—and die" (1 Kings 17:12).

Elijah's reply changed everything: "Don't be afraid. Go home and do as you have said. But first make a small loaf of bread for me from what you have and bring it to me, and then make something for yourself and your son. For this is what the LORD, the God of Israel, says:

> 'The jar of flour will not be used up and the jug of oil will not run dry until the day the LORD sends rain on the land'" (1 Kings 17:13-14).

One act of sacrificial faith unlocked ongoing provision. Every day afterward, the flour jar remained full. The oil never emptied. For months during famine, her kitchen supplied food for three people.

The widow heard God's voice through the prophet. She believed what seemed impossible. She obeyed despite her fear. She experienced God's faithfulness to His promise.

The Promise That Reframes Everything

God made you a concrete commitment:

> "And my God will meet all your needs according to the riches of his glory in Christ Jesus" (Phil. 4:19).

Every need. Not some. Not just spiritual ones. Every need of YOURS.

When God gave Israel His giving system, He embedded a promise:

> "Give generously to them and do so without a grudging heart; then because of this the LORD your God will bless you in all your work and in everything you put your hand to" (Deut. 15:10).

Notice the connection. YOUR generous giving → God's blessing on YOUR work. The provision for YOUR house follows the worship from YOUR heart.

God wants to bless YOUR work. He's promised to provide for YOUR needs. But He's waiting for you to ask—specifically.

When YOUR Math Doesn't Add Up

Renee stared at her bills again. The shortfall was exactly $644. Not an estimate—she calculated three times.

She thought about the widow of Zarephath. That woman had faced starvation with her last handful of flour. Renee wasn't starving, but she was desperate. The electric company's final notice wasn't a suggestion. The rent was already two days late.

During her morning quiet time, she'd been reading about specific prayers. The teaching wouldn't leave her mind: God responds to requests, not hints.

Renee pulled out a notepad and wrote: "God, I need $644 to cover the gap between my bills and income this month. I'm asking specifically because I trust You see my situation and care about my household."

Then she remembered the widow's faith step—giving her last meal to the prophet before God provided. Renee had $23 in cash—her emergency cushion for the week. Her elderly neighbor, Mrs. Thomas, had mentioned needing groceries but couldn't drive because of her knee surgery.

Renee felt the prompting clearly: *Give your emergency cushion to Mrs. Thomas, and then trust Me for your needs.*

She bought $20 worth of groceries—bread, milk, eggs, soup—and delivered them to Mrs. Thomas that afternoon.

"I can't afford this," Renee thought as she drove home. "But I also can't afford not to obey what I heard."

The Provision That Came Gradually

The first week, nothing happened. Renee checked her bank account daily. The numbers hadn't changed. On Tuesday night, she woke up at 2:47 AM in full panic mode.

"God, I'm scared. I need $644 and I have six days until the rent is officially late. I'm trusting You, but I'm scared."

No dramatic peace descended. Just her racing heart and the digital clock.

But provision started arriving through channels she hadn't expected.

Her former supervisor from the retail store where she worked three years ago texted: "Our inventory manager just quit. Can you help us catch up on back-office work? $25/hour, flexible schedule."

Renee worked twelve hours that week organizing their stockroom. After taxes: $240.

Mid-week two, her landlord knocked on her door. "I noticed you mentioned you used to do graphic design. My property management company needs someone to create flyers for our rentals. Would you be interested? I could pay you $200 for about six hours of work—and I'll waive that late fee since you're helping us out."

$200 more, plus the $50 late fee waived. Total now: $490.

Her ex-husband's child support check arrived two weeks late—$120. One of her home healthcare clients asked if she could work an extra shift—another $90. Her water bill refund from an overcharge three months ago finally processed—$48. She discovered she'd been miscalculating her electric bill—the amount due was $20 less than she thought.

Renee spread her calculations across the table:

- Retail inventory work: $240

- Graphic design: $200
- Late fee waived: $50
- Child support: $120
- Extra shift: $90
- Water refund: $48
- Electric correction: $20

Total: $768

She'd asked for $644. She'd received $768 through freelance work, skills she'd forgotten she had, payments arriving, and discovering she'd miscalculated.

Every bill was paid. The rent was current. The electricity stayed on. Groceries appeared on the table.

God had provided for HER house through means she hadn't orchestrated, at exactly the right time, through opportunities that used gifts she'd stopped thinking about.

Monique's Transportation Crisis

When Monique's fifteen-year-old car finally died, she needed reliable transportation for work and her kids' school, but she couldn't afford car payments on anything decent.

She prayed specifically: "God, I need reliable transportation for work and caring for my kids. Please provide what's best, not just what's cheapest."

Two weeks later, her supervisor—a believer she'd worked with for three years—mentioned he was upgrading to a new vehicle. "I've been wanting to sell my 2019 Honda to someone

I know will take care of it. I still owe $8,000 but it's worth about $12,000. I'd let you have it for $6,000 if you can get financing."

Monique had helped this supervisor through a difficult family situation the previous year, staying late multiple times to cover his shifts when his mother was hospitalized.

"I knew it was God," Monique said. "Not because money appeared from nowhere, but because the timing, the relationship, and the price all came together in ways I couldn't have arranged."

David's Specific Request

David's contracting business nearly collapsed during the 2008 recession. With three children and a mortgage, his savings disappeared within four months.

His wife suggested they stop tithing to focus on survival. David almost agreed—until he remembered the widow's oil story from a sermon.

They decided to keep giving while David prayed specifically: "God, I need three new contracts within sixty days to keep this business viable and our family fed."

Over the next six weeks, a former client called about emergency repairs after a pipe burst. A neighbor mentioned David's work to her parents, who needed kitchen renovation. His church asked him to bid on maintenance work for their building.

Three contracts in forty-two days. God answered his specific prayer through relationships he'd built, work he'd done well previously, and a church community that knew his character.

Not a dramatic miracle. Just faithful provision through ordinary channels at exactly the right time.

What Makes Prayer Powerful

Prayer moves heaven not because of perfect words, but because of three elements working together:

Specificity demonstrates faith. "God, I need $644 by the end of this month" shows more trust than "Please help my finances."

Sacrifice demonstrates trust. The widow gave her last meal. Renee gave her last $20. Small acts of obedience while waiting for provision demonstrate trust.

Persistence demonstrates belief. Renee's 2:47 AM panic didn't disqualify her prayer. Her choice to keep trusting despite fear mattered more.

The widow of Zarephath combined all three. She prayed through action (specific obedience), gave sacrificially (her last food), and trusted God's promise through the prophet even when it defied logic.

God provided for her household every single day for years.

He wants to provide for YOUR household too.

Questions for Your Heart

1. What specific financial need can you pray about right now instead of worrying?
2. How often do you make direct requests of God versus hinting at needs?
3. What small faith step could you take while waiting for provision?
4. How would your prayer life change if you believed God wants to answer your specific requests?

Prayer

Heavenly Father, I'm in my "handful of flour" moment. I'm scared but I choose to trust You like the widow did.

Right now, I specifically need [fill in exact need]. I'm asking directly as Your child who knows You own everything and promise to provide.

Thank You for [specific past provision]. Help me remember Your faithfulness when circumstances look impossible.

Show me what faith steps to take while I wait. Give me courage to obey what I hear from You. Let me experience Your provision in ways that build my faith and teach me to recognize Your voice more clearly.

I trust You to bless the work of MY hands. I believe Your promise to supply all MY needs. I'm listening for Your direction about MY household.

In Jesus' name, Amen.

Key Takeaway

When you pray specifically, give sacrificially, and trust completely, you position yourself to hear God's voice and experience His timely provision through means you didn't orchestrate—God's faithfulness to YOUR household may defy YOUR math, but it proves His promises about YOUR needs are absolutely reliable.

Chapter 10

When YOUR Husband Is God Himself

The pounding on Regina's door made her heart race. Through the peephole, she recognized the debt collector's uniform—the third visit this month.

Jason had died eight months ago. The heart attack in the Target parking lot came without warning. Cancer treatment for his brief illness had consumed their savings, maxed their credit cards, and mortgaged their future. The collectors wanted payment schedules, not sympathy for a grieving widow.

Regina had three children—ages six, nine, and eleven—a mortgage she couldn't afford, and monthly bills that multiplied faster than her limited income could address. She'd been a stay-at-home mom for twelve years. No recent work history. No career to return to. Just bills and three kids who needed stability.

The world looked at Regina and saw someone who had nothing. No husband. No career. No safety net. No options.

But the world was looking at the wrong ledger.

When "Having Nothing" Meant Certain Death

In the ancient world, widows occupied society's most desperate position. No job prospects, no legal rights to property, no career options. A widow's provision came through one source: her husband. When he died, she faced literal starvation unless family intervened.

When Scripture groups widows with orphans and foreigners, it's identifying society's most vulnerable—those with no advocate, no rights, no visible means of survival.

The world looked at widows and declared: "She has NOTHING."

But God saw something entirely different.

The Maker Who Becomes Husband

God spoke a radical promise through the prophet Isaiah to a nation that felt abandoned:

> "For your Maker is your husband—the LORD Almighty is his name—the Holy One of Israel is your Redeemer; he is called the God of all the earth" (Isa. 54:5).

Read that again slowly. YOUR MAKER IS YOUR HUSBAND.

This isn't a metaphor. This is God declaring: "When your earthly husband is gone, I AM YOUR HUSBAND NOW."

Not symbolically. Actually.

He takes the role of provider. Protector. Sustainer. Decision-maker. The One whose voice guides your household.

A married woman hears her husband's voice about finances: "I got the promotion." "The company is downsizing." "We can afford this." "We need to cut back." His voice shapes her household's provisions.

When that husband dies, God says: "NOW YOU HEAR MY VOICE."

Her security shifts from visible (earthly husband's paycheck) to invisible (heavenly Husband's provision). This requires learning to HEAR HIS VOICE where she once heard her husband's guidance.

Critical question: Will she HEAR His voice and TRUST His provision?

The Widow Who Heard God's Voice Through Famine

The worst drought in living memory had devastated Israel. No rain for three years. In Zarephath, a widow gathered sticks for one final task: cooking her last meal for herself and her son. After this, they would wait to die.

Then Elijah appeared, requesting water and bread.

Her response revealed desperation:

> "As surely as the LORD your God lives," she replied, "I don't have any bread—only a handful of flour in a jar and a little olive oil in a jug. I am gathering a few sticks to take

> home and make a meal for myself and my son, that we may eat it—and die" (1 Kings 17:12).

Elijah delivered God's message:

> "Don't be afraid. Go home and do as you have said. But first make a small loaf of bread for me from what you have and bring it to me, and then make something for yourself and your son. For this is what the LORD, the God of Israel, says: 'The jar of flour will not be used up and the jug of oil will not run dry until the day the LORD sends rain on the land'" (1 Kings 17:13-14).

Give your LAST FOOD to a stranger. Trust an invisible Provider when visible circumstances scream death.

> "She went away and did as Elijah had told her. So there was food every day for Elijah and for the woman and her family. For the jar of flour was not used up and the jug of oil did not run dry, in keeping with the word of the LORD spoken by Elijah" (1 Kings 17:15-16).

Daily provision for THREE YEARS during famine.

The Widow Who Heard God's Voice in Crisis

Another widow's husband had died leaving debt she couldn't

pay. Now the creditor was coming to take her two sons as slaves.

She ran to Elisha:

> "Your servant my husband is dead, and you know that he revered the LORD. But now his creditor is coming to take my two boys as his slaves" (2 Kings 4:1).

Elisha asked:

> "How can I help you? Tell me, what do you have in your house?"
> "Your servant has nothing there at all," she said, "except a small jar of olive oil" (2 Kings 4:2).

God's voice came through the prophet:

> "Go around and ask all your neighbors for empty jars. Don't ask for just a few. Then go inside and shut the door behind you and your sons. Pour oil into all the jars, and as each is filled, put it to one side" (2 Kings 4:3-4).

She obeyed. The oil flowed until she ran out of containers. Elisha told her:

> "Go, sell the oil and pay your debts. You and your sons can live on what is left" (2 Kings 4:7).

Not just enough—OVERFLOW.

The Widow Who Heard God's Voice in Worship

Jesus watched people contribute offerings at the temple treasury. Rich donors approached with conspicuous generosity. Then a widow withdrew two small copper coins—the smallest denominations available, together worth a fraction of a penny. Everything she had.

Jesus called His disciples:

> "Truly I tell you, this poor widow has put more into the treasury than all the others. They all gave out of their wealth; but she, out of her poverty, put in everything—all she had to live on" (Mark 12:43-44).

She gave what she needed for food. What she needed for survival. Everything. She was declaring: "My Maker is my Husband. He will provide for tomorrow."

All three widows demonstrate the same pattern: HEAR God's voice → BELIEVE His promise → OBEY His direction → EXPERIENCE His provision.

Regina's Impossible Math

Three months after Jason died, the insurance money was running out. Regina sat on her couch late one Tuesday night, trying to make the numbers work.

Her mother had suggested moving back home to Ohio. "You

can't afford to stay in Phoenix. Come home. We'll help with the kids."

Regina understood the logic. But uprooting her children from their schools, their friends, their home—right after losing their father—felt wrong. She'd prayed about it for weeks. Every time, she felt the same thing: *Stay. Trust Me.*

But staying required money she didn't have.

The Morning God Spoke About the Spare Room

That same week, Regina was reading her Bible during early morning quiet time. She'd opened up to 2 Kings—the story of Elisha and the widow whose oil multiplied.

She read:

> "Elisha replied to her, 'How can I help you? Tell me, what do you have in your house?'" (2 Kings 4:2).

The question captured her: *What do you have in your house?*

She walked through the house, really looking. Four bedrooms. Three kids. Jason's home office, mostly unused now. The spare bedroom—the "guest room" even though guests rarely came.

Standing in that doorway, Regina heard something. Not audible. But clear: *Rent this room to traveling nurses.*

The thought wouldn't leave. *Traveling nurses need short-term housing. You have a spare room.*

Regina spent that day researching. She discovered an entire industry of traveling healthcare workers who took temporary assignments and needed housing for 8–16-week contracts.

"What you have in your house" suddenly made sense.

But doubt crept in. Who would choose to live with a grieving widow and three children?

Then, during prayer: *Trust Me. I'm your Provider now. Do you believe that?*

Regina created a simple listing on a website for traveling nurses. She priced it at $800 per month—enough to cover a significant portion of her mortgage.

Three days passed. No response.

Monday morning, an email arrived: "Hi, I'm Bethany. I'm a travel nurse starting a 12-week assignment at Banner Hospital next month. Your listing looks perfect."

Bethany would arrive in three weeks. Regina hung up, stunned. In three weeks, she'd have $800 monthly income from a room that had been sitting empty.

Learning to Hear Her Maker-Husband's Voice

Six months after Jason died, Regina's friend suggested she stop tithing until she got "financially stable."

That Sunday, her pastor preached from Isaiah 54:5: "Your Maker is your husband."

Something shifted in Regina's understanding. Not "God will help you" but "God wants to BE your provider now."

Like the widows in Scripture, she needed to learn how to HEAR HIS VOICE about finances.

Monday morning during prayer, she sensed God clearly: "KEEP GIVING. I'M YOUR HUSBAND NOW."

The following Sunday, Regina contemplated as she wrote her regular tithe check. This felt foolish. But she'd heard God's voice—about the spare room, about staying in Phoenix, about giving.

Eighteen Months Later

Over the next eighteen months, five different traveling healthcare workers rented Regina's spare room. Each stayed 10-16 weeks. Each time, God provided the next renter with minimal gap between guests.

The spare room income—$800 monthly when occupied—made the impossible possible. Mortgage payments became manageable. Her kids' stability remained intact.

But the deeper transformation was internal. Regina was learning daily what it meant for God to be her Provider-Husband.

Where Jason had once discussed finances with her, God now spoke through provision that appeared in His timing. She learned to hear His voice through Scripture during morning devotions. Through peace about decisions that didn't make logical sense. Through specific directions about using what she already had.

When her car registration came due and she didn't have the full amount, she prayed. The next day, her mother-in-law called with Jason's company life insurance payout—$1,200, the exact amount needed.

When her daughter needed dental work insurance didn't cover, she brought it to God. Within a week, a forgotten tax refund arrived—$340, enough for the co-pay.

She wasn't experiencing windfalls. She was experiencing provision. Timely. Specific. Through means she hadn't orchestrated.

The Question That Changes Your Crisis

When you're facing impossible financial circumstances, God asks the same question He asked the widow:

"What do you have in your house?"

Not what you wish you had. Not what you used to have. What do YOU have right now that God could use for YOUR provision?

Maybe it's a skill you've stopped using. Maybe it's space you're not utilizing. Maybe it's time you could redirect. Maybe it's knowledge you could share.

God specializes in using what YOU already have to provide for YOUR specific needs—when YOU hear His voice and obey His direction.

Regina's spare room wasn't dramatic. It wasn't a miracle windfall. It was simply using what she already possessed in a way God directed—creating ongoing provision that sustained her household month after month.

God promises:

> "And the peace of God, which transcends all understanding, will guard your hearts and your minds in Christ Jesus" (Phil. 4:7).

This peace doesn't depend on having enough money. It depends on knowing the One who owns everything.

God isn't promising you'll never face financial storms. He's promising you'll never face them alone:

> "Never will I leave you; never will I forsake you" (Heb. 13:5).

Questions for Your Heart

1. What specific financial worry has been stealing YOUR sleep most consistently?
2. When has God provided for YOU in ways you never calculated or anticipated?
3. What do YOU have in YOUR house that God might be directing you to use for provision—a spare room, a skill, knowledge, time, space?
4. Are you living as if God is YOUR Provider-Husband, or are you panicking as if you're alone?

Prayer

Heavenly Father, I confess that financial anxiety has been stealing my peace. I've been calculating as if I'm alone, forgetting that You're with me.

Help me remember that You specialize in calming storms I can't control. When I'm tempted to panic at midnight, remind me to thank You instead.

Show me what I have in my house that You could use for my provision. Open my eyes to resources I'm overlooking, opportunities I'm dismissing, or assets I'm underutilizing.

Break the grip that money has on my heart. Replace my financial anxiety with faith-filled trust in Your presence. You've never left me. You've never forsaken me. You're with me right now.

Thank You for YOUR perfect track record of providing for me. Help me to trust You as my Provider-Husband.

In Jesus' name, Amen.

Key Takeaway

When YOUR earthly provider is gone, YOU are perfectly positioned to hear God's voice as YOUR Maker-Husband who promises to provide for YOUR household—often by asking "What do you have in your house?" and directing you to use what you already possess to generate provision through obedience to His voice.

Chapter 11

When YOUR Employer Breaks Promises

Sheila walks into her supervisor's office expecting a routine quarterly review. Instead, she receives news that makes her stomach drop:

"We're restructuring your compensation package."

Translation: She's getting paid less for identical work.

The commission structure she'd built her budget around? "Adjusted downward for market conditions." The raise promised during her last performance review? "Delayed indefinitely due to budget constraints." The bonus structure that had motivated her to exceed targets? "Modified to reflect new company priorities."

Sheila forces a professional smile while calculating the impact. Rent, car payment, student loans—everything depended on income that just evaporated through corporate restructuring.

She's in excellent company.

The Uncle Who Redefined Workplace Injustice

Jacob understood exactly how Sheila felt. For twenty years, he worked for his uncle Laban, experiencing compensation manipulation that would violate every modern labor law.

Every. Single. Change. Benefited. Laban.

Years 1-7: "Work seven years and marry my daughter Rachel." Jacob worked exceptionally. The wedding day arrived. Laban substituted daughters. "Wrong girl. Work seven MORE years for Rachel."

Years 8-14: Jacob worked another seven years, finally marrying Rachel.

Years 15-20: "Now work for livestock as wages." Laban kept modifying arrangements to benefit himself exclusively.

The Bible records Jacob's complaint:

> "Your father has cheated me by changing my wages ten times" (Gen. 31:7).

Ten times. Twenty years. One dishonest employer.

The Vow That Started It All

Before Jacob ever met Laban, something remarkable happened during his desperate flight from Esau's anger.

Sleeping outdoors with stones for pillows, Jacob received an extraordinary vision: angels ascending and descending a ladder connecting heaven and earth. God Himself making incredible promises about land, descendants, protection, and provision.

Jacob's response proved pivotal:

> "If God will be with me and will watch over me on this journey I am taking and will give me food to eat and clothes to wear so that I return safely to my father's household, then the LORD will be my God and this stone that I have set up as a pillar will be God's house, and of all that you give me I will give you a tenth" (Gen. 28:20-22).

History's second recorded commitment to return the tenth to God. Not because God demanded it, but because Jacob wanted to honor the God who promised provision.

The Supernatural Multiplication Under Oppression

Twenty years later, Jacob's employment with Laban became a systematic exploitation. But something incredible happened: the more Laban tried cheating Jacob, the more Jacob prospered.

Scripture clearly condemns wage theft:

> "Do not hold back the wages of a hired worker overnight" (Lev. 19:13).

God hates employer dishonesty. While Laban schemed, God worked supernaturally.

Jacob's flocks multiplied beyond natural breeding patterns. His wealth grew despite Laban's manipulations. The harder Laban tried cheating him, the more God blessed him through miraculous increase.

Finally, God spoke to Jacob in a dream:

> "I am the God of Bethel, where you anointed a pillar and where you made a vow to me. Now leave this land at once and go back to your native land" (Gen. 31:13).

God had monitored the entire situation. Every unfair wage reduction. Every broken promise. Every manipulative tactic.

He kept detailed records and provided supernatural compensation.

Divine Intervention in Modern Workplaces: My Story

I discovered this principle directly while working for a large company. Six months into the job, I overheard two coworkers casually discussing salary adjustments. They were making $10,000 more per year than me—same job, same qualifications, different paychecks.

The injustice hit hard. That was mortgage payments, childcare costs, and groceries. But as I sat calculating what that money could have covered, I heard God's voice clearly: *Don't get caught up in the complaining and gossip. Trust Me.*

That evening, my wife asked a question that shifted my perspective: "What did you hear from God about it?"

"He told me to trust Him instead of focusing on the unfairness," I admitted.

"Then maybe this is about more than the salary," she said.

The Decision Despite Impossible Math

Around that same time, teaching at church about returning the tithe—that first tenth that belongs to the Lord—wouldn't leave us alone.

Looking at our budget, the numbers were brutal. Our expenses exceeded our income even before considering the tenth.

"What do we have to lose?" my wife asked. "We don't have enough anyway. Maybe it's time to actually trust what we've been hearing."

We made the decision that night: we would return to God what belongs to Him despite the workplace injustice, despite the impossible math. Because God was asking us to trust Him as our source, not our employer.

From Nervous Obedience to Unexpected Peace

The first three months were hard. Every time I wrote that check, my hand would hesitate. "This could pay for groceries," I'd think.

But by month six, something remarkable happened. I wrote the check without hesitation. Sitting with my wife that evening, I said, "Did you notice we're not panicking about money anymore?"

We didn't miss what we'd been returning to God. The 90% was somehow covering what 100% hadn't covered before—not through magical multiplication, but through deep peace that we would be okay because we were trusting God.

God's Creative Provision

About eight months in, I learned about the company's suggestion system for process improvements. I'd never paid attention before, but suddenly I was noticing opportunities. I submitted two suggestions. Both were approved, bringing unexpected compensation.

Around the same time, my wife started providing childcare for neighborhood families. The income wasn't huge, but it made a difference.

Neither income source had anything to do with my employer. God was providing through channels we hadn't even considered.

Over the next two years, I started getting raises. I wasn't complaining or spreading gossip—just working with excellence and trusting God. After a couple of years, my salary had increased by about $12,000.

I'd begun $10,000 behind my colleagues. Several years later, I was ahead of where they'd been. God had not only made up the difference—He'd exceeded it.

The Lesson That Changed Everything

That season taught me to trust God as my source, not my

employer. My employer determined my salary, but God determined my provision.

Workplace injustice can't limit God's provision when you're returning to Him what belongs to Him. The suggestion system and my wife's childcare income weren't on our radar when we first made the decision. God opened channels we didn't know existed.

Most importantly, peace in finances doesn't come from having enough money—it comes from trusting the right Source.

The Mathematics That Defy Human Logic

Jacob's experience—and mine—teaches foundational principles about divine economics:

> Your employer determines your salary. God determines your provision.

Laban could manipulate Jacob's wages, but he couldn't manipulate God's blessing. When you return to God what belongs to Him—especially through consistent faithfulness with the tenth—you declare:

- "God, You're my ultimate provider"
- "I trust You more than my paycheck"
- "I believe You can provide beyond my employer's limitations"

This kind of faith activates supernatural provision that transcends human workplace politics.

Sophia's Gift Turned Business: When Skills Become Income

Sophia worked as an administrative assistant when her company announced sudden layoffs. After eight years of loyal service, she received two weeks' severance and a form letter thanking her for her contributions.

The panic hit immediately. She was a single mother with a mortgage and a daughter starting college in six months. Her modest salary had barely covered expenses—now she had nothing.

But during her final week at the office, she remembered Jacob's story from a Bible study months earlier. Twenty years of wage manipulation, yet God provided supernaturally.

"God," Sophia prayed that night, "I don't understand why this happened, but I'm choosing to trust You. I'll keep returning what belongs to You even though I don't know where next month's income is coming from."

Her sister thought she was crazy. "Sophia, you just lost your job. You need every dollar for the mortgage. Stop giving until you're back on your feet."

But Sophia sensed God's voice clearly: *Keep trusting. Honor Me. I'm about to show you something.*

The Skill She'd Been Giving Away

For years, Sophia had a gift for organizing spaces. Friends constantly asked her to help declutter their homes, organize their closets, set up their home offices. She always said yes—never charging, just helping because she enjoyed it.

Three days after losing her job, a neighbor knocked on her door. "Sophia, I know you're between positions right now. I'm moving my elderly mother into assisted living and need help organizing her belongings. It's overwhelming. Would you be willing to help? I can pay you."

Sophia agreed, thinking it would be a one-time project.

The job took three days. The neighbor paid her $600. As Sophia was finishing, the neighbor's friend stopped by and saw the transformation. "Could you help me? I've been trying to organize my basement for two years."

That weekend, Sophia organized the basement. Another $400.

God's Business Idea

Monday morning during prayer, Sophia felt God speaking clearly: *This is how I'm going to provide. Turn your gift into a business.*

She'd never considered professional organizing as a career. It was just something she enjoyed doing for friends. But as she prayed, the idea wouldn't leave her mind.

Within a week, Sophia created a simple website: "Sophia's Organizing Solutions." She listed her services, posted before-and-after photos from the two projects (with permission), and shared it on social media.

Her first client came from church—someone who'd watched her organize the children's ministry supply closet months earlier. Then a friend's coworker. Then a referral from the basement project.

By month three, Sophia was booked two weeks out. She was earning more per month than her administrative assistant salary—and she controlled her own schedule, which meant she could attend her daughter's college orientation without asking permission.

"God didn't just replace my job," Sophia told her small group six months later. "He showed me a gift I'd been using for free could provide for my household. I'd been giving away what He wanted me to use for provision. When my employer let me go, God revealed what He'd been preparing me for all along."

The Promise for YOUR Work

God made a specific commitment about YOUR work and YOUR provision:

> "Give generously to them and do so without a grudging heart; then because of this the LORD your God will bless you in all your work and in everything you put your hand to" (Deut. 15:10).

Notice what God promises:

- He will bless YOU
- In all YOUR work
- In everything YOU put YOUR hand to

This isn't generic. It's personal. YOUR work. YOUR hands. YOUR provision.

When you honor God by returning what belongs to Him—especially when you feel underpaid, undervalued, or treated unfairly—you activate this promise. God takes responsibility for blessing the work of YOUR hands.

Your Response to Workplace Injustice

Instead of fighting your employer's unfairness, start trusting God's faithfulness through these steps:

This Week:

- Calculate the tenth and commit to returning it to God consistently
- Declare out loud: "God, You are my provider, not my employer"
- Work with excellence regardless of how you're treated
- Pray specifically about your workplace situation instead of complaining

This Month:

- Maintain faithful returning of what belongs to God despite feeling underpaid
- Watch for God's provision through unexpected sources
- Document any unusual opportunities or favor you experience

- Trust God's timing rather than forcing solutions

This Quarter:

- Expect doors opening that your employer cannot control
- Notice how God's provision comes through various channels
- Build relationships that could lead to better opportunities
- Trust God's supernatural mathematics over human calculations

The Principle That Changes Everything

Jacob returned the tenth to God. He honored God financially despite workplace injustice. God provided supernaturally—multiplication that Laban couldn't stop.

I returned the tenth to God. I honored God financially despite being underpaid. God provided creatively—through suggestion systems, through my wife's childcare income, through raises I wasn't pursuing.

Sophia returned the tenth to God. She honored God financially despite job loss. God revealed a gift-based business—turning skills she'd given away for free into income that exceeded her former salary.

The pattern is consistent:

> Your employer determines your salary. God determines your provision.

When God becomes your source, no employer can truly underpay you.

Questions for YOUR Heart

1. How has your employer's unfairness affected your trust in God's provision?
    1. What would change if you truly believed God controls your career advancement more than your supervisor does?
    2. How could you demonstrate trust in God as your provider this week, regardless of workplace circumstances?
    3. What practical step will you take to honor God financially despite feeling underpaid?

Prayer

Heavenly Father, I feel undervalued and underpaid at work, but I choose to trust You as my ultimate provider. Help me honor You by faithfully returning what belongs to You even when the mathematics seem impossible.

Give me strength to work excellently despite unfair treatment. Open doors of opportunity and provision that no employer can shut. Show me that my security comes from Your character, not my paycheck.

When workplace injustice creates bitterness or anxiety, remind me of Jacob's experience and help me trust Your timing. Use my current circumstances to position me for the opportunities You have prepared.

Multiply my faithfulness supernaturally. Help me remember: my employer determines my salary, but You determine my provision.

In Jesus' name, Amen.

Key Takeaway

Your employer determines your salary, but God determines your provision. When you honor God by faithfully returning what belongs to Him—especially during workplace injustice—you activate His promise to bless the work of YOUR hands. No employer's unfairness can limit what God wants to provide when you're trusting Him as your ultimate source.

Chapter 12

When YOUR Small Gifts Trigger Big Provision

The disciples calculated the problem: five thousand hungry people, no food available, miles from any town. Their solution seemed obvious—send everyone away to buy their own food.

But a boy had packed lunch that morning. Five barley loaves and two small fish. Andrew brought him to Jesus, asking the question everyone wondered:

> "Here is a boy with five small barley loaves and two small fish, but how far will they go among so many?" (John 6:9).

Not far by human calculation. But in Jesus' hands, that inadequate lunch fed five thousand men, plus women and children, with twelve baskets of leftovers.

God specializes in multiplying what seems embarrassingly small when YOU offer it in faith for YOUR provision.

Cynthia's Resume Gap

Cynthia opened the rejection email, her seventeenth in four months. "We've decided to move forward with other candidates."

She'd worked as an accountant for eight years before her twin daughters were born. Five years at home raising them. Now, trying to return to the workforce at forty-two, her resume gaps felt like disqualifications no one would overlook.

The math was simple and terrifying: Her husband's income covered about 70% of their household expenses. They needed her to bring in at least $2,000 monthly to stay current on bills. Without it, they'd fall behind on the mortgage within three months.

"God, I need a job," she prayed during morning quiet time. "Any job. Just something to help us make it."

She kept reading her Bible plan: the feeding of five thousand. One phrase stood out to her: the boy gave what he had, not what he wished he had.

What do YOU have that YOU could offer?

She had accounting skills. Current certifications. Eight years of experience. But apparently, that wasn't what employers wanted—not with five years away from the profession.

The thought wouldn't leave her: *What if YOU stopped trying to get someone to hire YOU and started using what's already in YOUR hands?*

The Voice That Redirected Her Skills

Wednesday morning, Cynthia sat with her computer looking at job boards for the hundredth time. Nothing she qualified for. Nothing that would hire someone with her gaps.

Then she thought about her friend Lisa who'd mentioned her frustration with her small retail boutique's bookkeeping. "I can't afford a full-time accountant, and the software confuses me."

Lisa couldn't afford full-time help. But what if she didn't need full-time help? What if Cynthia could do her books remotely for a few hours each week?

The idea felt small. Part-time virtual bookkeeping wasn't the full-time position she'd been praying for. It wasn't a salary with benefits. It was just... using what she had differently.

But the thought persisted: *Offer what YOU have. Trust Me for what YOU need.*

Thursday afternoon, Cynthia texted Lisa: "Remember you mentioned needing bookkeeping help? I could do your books remotely—maybe 4-5 hours a week. Would that interest you?"

Lisa called within an hour. "Yes! What would you charge?"

Cynthia calculated quickly: 5 hours weekly at $25/hour would be $500 monthly. "Five hundred a month?"

"That's less than my last accountant, and you'd actually organize everything? When can you start?"

The Provision That Built Gradually

Cynthia started with Lisa's boutique in October. Five hours weekly, $500 monthly. Not the $2,000 they needed, but it was something.

The next week, Lisa mentioned Cynthia's help to another small business owner. "She handles my books remotely, and it's affordable. You should talk to her."

Michael owned a small electrical contracting business. Same problem—books were a mess, couldn't afford full-time help, needed someone to make sense of the financial chaos.

Cynthia took him on. Six hours weekly, $600 monthly.

In November, Michael referred her to a consulting firm that needed quarterly reports prepared. Four hours monthly, $400 total.

December brought two more small clients through referrals: a home staging company ($300 monthly) and a property management firm ($200 monthly).

By January, Cynthia had five clients totaling $2,000 monthly—the exact amount they'd needed to cover their household gap.

Not from the full-time job she'd been praying for, but from using her "inadequate" skills in ways she hadn't imagined.

Small Gifts in Unexpected Places

Vanessa sat in her car outside the dollar store with $2.47—literally everything she had until her paycheck arrived in three days.

Her six-year-old daughter Sophia bounced in the backseat. "Mama, can we go in? I want to pick something for Mrs. Johnson!"

Tomorrow, other parents would arrive at school with elaborate gifts and generous gift cards. Vanessa had $2.47.

Inside, Sophia picked up a small vanilla-scented candle. $1.25. "This one. Mrs. Johnson loves vanilla. And vanilla smells like cookies, and cookies make people happy!"

They added a greeting card ($1.00) and a candy cane ($0.22). Total: $2.47.

The next morning, Mrs. Johnson received gifts from twenty-three students. Gift cards to Target, Starbucks, Amazon. Expensive lotions. A Michael Kors bag from one wealthy family.

Then Sophia presented her candle and card.

Mrs. Johnson read the card aloud: "Dear Mrs. Johnson, You are the best teacher. You make learning fun. This candle smells like vanilla and vanilla smells like cookies and cookies make people happy. I hope this makes you happy. Love, Sophia."

Mrs. Johnson knelt beside Sophia's desk, pulling her into a hug. "Thank you so much, sweetheart. This is perfect."

Two days later, an email arrived: "Dear Ms. Rodriguez, I wanted you to know how much Sophia's gift meant to me. I received many generous presents, but hers touched my heart in a special way... Your daughter's simple gift reminded me why I became a teacher."

Three months later, when Sophia struggled with math, Mrs. Johnson stayed after school twice a week for a month helping her—refusing payment, saying simply, "Sophia's gift to me was priceless. This is my gift back."

Sophia's two-dollar candle had created something money

couldn't buy—a relationship that blessed her daughter throughout that school year.

The Promise for YOUR Work

God made a specific commitment about YOUR work and YOUR provision:

> "Give generously to them and do so without a grudging heart; then because of this the LORD your God will bless you in all your work and in everything you put your hand to" (Deut. 15:10).

Notice what God promises:

- He will bless YOU
- In all YOUR work
- In everything YOU put YOUR hand to

This isn't generic. It's personal. YOUR work. YOUR hands. YOUR provision.

Cynthia's accounting skills seemed inadequate for landing full-time employment. But they were perfect for serving five small businesses who needed affordable bookkeeping—creating exactly the $2,000 monthly her household required.

Sophia's $2.47 seemed inadequate for a teacher gift. But it created a relationship that blessed her education in ways expensive gifts never could.

The boy's lunch wasn't inadequate—it just needed Jesus' hands to multiply it. Cynthia's skills weren't inadequate—they just needed to be offered where God directed. Vanessa's $2.47 wasn't inadequate—it just needed Sophia's thoughtful heart to make it meaningful.

God provides for YOUR house through means YOU didn't calculate. YOUR small offerings in God's hands become HIS provision for YOUR household needs.

Questions for YOUR Heart

1. What "small gift" have YOU been embarrassed to offer because it seems inadequate for YOUR needs?
2. What skills or resources do YOU have that haven't worked in traditional ways—could they work differently to provide for YOUR household?
3. How has focusing on what YOU lack prevented YOU from using what YOU have for YOUR provision?
4. What if God is waiting for YOUR small offering before releasing HIS multiplication for YOUR household?

Prayer

God, I feel embarrassed by what I have to offer. My gifts seem so small compared to what I need. My skills haven't worked the way I expected. My resume has gaps. My resources are limited.

But I'm choosing to believe that YOU specialize in multiplying what seems embarrassingly inadequate when I offer it in faith.

Help me see that my small gifts matter to YOU—and that YOU can multiply them for MY household provision.

Show me if I'm trying to use good gifts in wrong ways. Give me creativity to see how my skills, time, or resources could serve differently than I've imagined. Help me hear YOUR voice about using what I already have in ways I haven't considered.

I trust YOU to provide for MY household through means I haven't calculated. Take my small offering and multiply it beyond my expectations.

In Jesus' name, Amen.

Key Takeaway

God specializes in multiplying small gifts YOU offer in faith to provide for YOUR household—YOUR accounting skills that haven't landed traditional employment, YOUR two-dollar candle, YOUR limited resources become more than adequate when YOU give what YOU have rather than waiting until YOU have more, willing to use YOUR gifts differently than YOU planned.

Chapter 13

The Treasure Test That Reveals YOUR Heart

When Sarah died after sixty-seven years of marriage, Abraham needed burial land. He approached Ephron the Hittite about purchasing the cave of Machpelah.

Ephron offered the land as a gift in front of the entire community:

> "No, my lord," he said. "Listen to me; I give you the field, and I give you the cave that is in it. I give it to you in the presence of my people. Bury your dead" (Gen. 23:11).

A generous gesture witnessed by everyone. Free prime real estate for burying his beloved wife.

Abraham refused.

> "Listen to me, if you will. I will pay the price of the field. Accept it from me so I can bury my dead there" (Gen. 23:13).

Ephron named his price: four hundred shekels of silver—equivalent to roughly $50,000 in today's currency—an enormous sum.

Abraham paid it immediately. Full price. No negotiation. No discount.

Why reject free land? Because Abraham understood something crucial: What costs you nothing means nothing to you.

Abraham paid an enormous amount because this burial site mattered eternally. His costly purchase revealed where his heart resided—not in accumulating wealth, but in honoring what mattered forever.

The purchase became sacred ground where Sarah, Abraham, Isaac, Rebekah, Leah, and Jacob would all be buried. That $50,000 investment secured the family's eternal resting place and demonstrated to all future generations what Abraham truly treasured.

The Diagnostic That Never Lies

Jesus provided a test to reveal where your heart actually resides:

> "For where your treasure is, there your heart will be also" (Matt. 6:21).

Your treasure isn't what you claim matters most. It's what you actually invest in most consistently.

Want to know what you truly treasure? Don't listen to what you say on Sunday morning. Look at your bank statements and calendar for the past three months.

Where does your money go? Where does your time go? That reveals your real treasure.

Because here's the truth: You don't treasure what you invest in. You invest in what you treasure.

The Rich Man's Treasure Tragedy

A wealthy young ruler approached Jesus seeking eternal life. He confidently listed his religious credentials:

> "All these I have kept since I was a boy" (Mark 10:20).

He'd followed the commandments. Attended religious services. Lived morally. Done everything right according to external standards.

Jesus looked at him and loved him. Then He identified what actually owned this man's heart:

> "Go, sell everything you have and give to the poor, and you will have treasure in heaven. Then come, follow me" (Mark 10:21).

The Bible records his response with devastating simplicity:

> "At this the man's face fell. He went away sad, because he had great wealth" (Mark 10:22).

Jesus had pinpointed his functional god: money. To follow Jesus authentically, he needed to abandon what truly ruled his life.

He chose his treasure over Jesus. His treasure revealed his heart. His heart determined his eternal destiny.

The tragedy wasn't that he had wealth. The tragedy was that wealth had him.

Adrienne's $200,000 Test

Adrienne had spent eight years building her marketing agency from nothing. She'd started in her apartment with one freelance client, working nights and weekends while holding down a day job. Eventually she quit to focus on the agency full-time—a terrifying decision that required maxing out credit cards.

By year eight, she had four employees and was earning enough to pay herself a decent salary and start saving for the first time.

Then the $200,000 contract appeared.

A financial services company approached her about a year-long marketing campaign. The largest contract her agency had ever seen.

Adrienne met with their team, reviewed their materials, and felt increasing unease.

The company targeted elderly populations with complex financial products designed to maximize fees while minimizing transparency. Their marketing materials used confusing language intentionally. Their sales tactics pressured seniors into products they didn't understand. The whole operation felt predatory.

But $200,000. For one year of work. That would cover her entire payroll, her office lease, and her own salary with room left over.

She took the contract home.

That weekend, she showed the materials to her husband. "This feels wrong. Look at this language. It's deliberately confusing. They're pushing 78-year-old widows into high-risk investments."

Her husband read through the documents. "You're right. This is predatory." He looked at her. "But Adrienne, we're talking about $200,000."

"I know."

The contract sat on Adrienne's desk for three weeks. She looked at it every morning. Calculated what $200,000 would mean for her agency. Imagined the financial security it would provide.

Her accountant's response was immediate: "Take it. You can't save the world. Your responsibility is business viability. This ensures your agency survives another year. That's the ethical choice."

But every time she read through the client's materials, she felt that unease intensify. She started praying about it.

"God, what am I supposed to do? We need this money. But I feel sick every time I imagine creating campaigns that hurt vulnerable people."

She kept waiting for clear direction. Instead, she just felt that persistent, quiet conviction: *This isn't right. You know this isn't right.*

Week three, Adrienne had lunch with her pastor. The contract came up.

"It's $200,000," she said. "How do I walk away from that?"

Her pastor was quiet for a moment. "What's the treasure test revealing? Where your treasure is, your heart is also. Right now, what are you treasuring? The money or your integrity?"

That conversation settled it.

Adrienne emailed the financial services company that afternoon: "After careful consideration, I don't believe our agency is the right fit for your marketing needs. I'm declining the contract."

She closed her laptop and felt something she hadn't expected: peace.

The Hard Months

The next three months were hard. No major contracts materialized. She paid employees from her line of credit. She stopped paying herself. Her husband picked up extra shifts. They cancelled their vacation.

By month four, Adrienne started wondering if she'd misheard God. Maybe she could have taken the money and used it for good.

Month six brought a phone call from a nonprofit she'd done work for two years earlier. "We've been awarded a major grant.

Part of our funding is designated for professional marketing. We immediately thought of you."

The nonprofit's contract wasn't as large as the predatory company's offer—$85,000 instead of $200,000. But it was for work Adrienne felt genuinely good about: helping an organization that provided financial literacy education to low-income families.

Over the next three months, two more opportunities arrived: an ethical investment firm ($67,000) and a sustainable business consulting firm ($73,000).

By year's end, Adrienne's agency had brought in $225,000 in revenue—more than the predatory contract would have paid. But more importantly, every client represented work she felt good about.

"I learned something," Adrienne told her husband. "Those six months of wondering if I'd made a terrible mistake? That was the treasure test continuing. Would I keep trusting Him even when provision didn't come right away? Or would I regret choosing integrity over money?"

"I'd make the same choice again. Because now I know what I actually treasure. And it's not the biggest paycheck."

Two Kinds of Treasure

Jesus made the choice clear:

> "Do not store up for yourselves treasures on earth, where moths and vermin destroy, and where thieves break in and steal. But store

> up for yourselves treasures in heaven, where moths and vermin do not destroy, and where thieves do not break in and steal. For where your treasure is, there your heart will be also" (Matt. 6:19-21).

Earth rewards are temporary—money that can be lost, success that fades, approval that changes. Heaven rewards are eternal —recognition from God, treasure that never disappears, joy that never ends.

Abraham paid $50,000 for burial land because he treasured eternal significance over temporary wealth. That purchase became sacred ground for generations.

The rich young ruler walked away sad because he treasured temporary wealth over eternal significance. He's remembered forever as the man who chose wrong.

Adrienne turned down $200,000 because she treasured integrity over immediate financial security. God honored that choice with aligned clients and peaceful conscience.

Jesus promises:

> "And everyone who has left houses or brothers or sisters or father or mother or wife or children or fields for my sake will receive a hundred times as much and will inherit eternal life" (Matt. 19:29).

The rewards aren't always financial. Sometimes they're relational peace, clear conscience, joy in work, purpose in service, freedom from money's grip, or simply knowing you chose correctly.

But the promise is real: What you sacrifice for eternal treasure, God multiplies in ways that matter forever.

Questions for YOUR Heart

1. What does YOUR treasure audit reveal about where YOUR heart actually resides? (Look at your bank statements, calendar, and what occupies your thoughts)
2. What would be most difficult for YOU to sacrifice for eternal treasure?
3. What practical step will YOU take this week to relocate YOUR treasure from earth to heaven?
4. If YOU lost everything you currently treasure most, would YOU still have peace knowing God remains?

Prayer

Jesus, search my heart and show me what I'm treasuring more than You. Give me courage to relocate my treasure from temporary things to eternal things, regardless of what it costs.

Help me see that You're worth any sacrifice I might make. When counting the cost feels overwhelming, help me also count the cost of NOT following You completely.

Change my heart from someone who wants easy blessings to someone willing to invest everything in Your kingdom. Show me through honest examination of MY time, money, and energy where MY treasure really lies.

Make MY life prove that following You is worth whatever earthly treasure I might sacrifice for eternal reward.

In Your name, Amen.

Key Takeaway

YOUR treasure reveals where YOUR heart truly resides—examine YOUR bank statements, YOUR calendar, and YOUR mental energy to discover what YOU actually treasure, then choose courage to sacrifice temporary wealth for eternal significance, trusting God's promise that following Jesus provides rewards exceeding any temporal sacrifice.

Chapter 14

Is He Worth It?

The Disciples' Bold Question

Peter had followed Jesus for three years. He'd abandoned his fishing business, missed significant income opportunities, and faced rejection from religious leaders who disapproved of Jesus.

One day, Peter asked Jesus the ultimate question:

> "We have left everything to follow you! What then will there be for us?" (Matt. 19:27).

Translation: "Jesus, we've sacrificed substantially. Is it worth it? What do we actually get?"

Instead of rebuking Peter's honest question, Jesus gave an incredible answer:

> "Everyone who has left houses or brothers or sisters or father or mother or wife or children or fields for my sake will receive a hundred times as much and will inherit eternal life" (Matt. 19:29).

Jesus wasn't offended by cost-benefit analysis. He understood that following Him requires sacrifice, and people need assurance the rewards are real.

Marcus's Crisis: When Success Costs Your Soul

Marcus had worked in pharmaceutical sales for nine years, earning $104,000 annually. His family lived comfortably. His wife Jennifer stayed home with their two kids, ages eight and eleven. Life was good.

And he was becoming increasingly sick about how he earned that success.

Marcus had entered pharmaceutical sales attracted by earning potential and the promise of helping people access life-improving medications. But as his career advanced, ethical lines blurred. His company launched medications costing significantly more than equally effective alternatives. His compensation structure heavily incentivized promoting expensive options over cheaper generics—even when clinical data showed minimal difference in outcomes.

By year nine, he was a top regional performer earning over $120,000 with bonuses.

And he'd developed an ulcer from suppressing his conscience.

The Awakening

The moment Marcus could no longer ignore what he'd become happened on a Tuesday afternoon in November.

He was waiting in Dr. Kowalski's office lobby when he overheard a conversation at the check-out window. An elderly woman—Mrs. Patterson—was speaking with the office manager about her prescriptions.

"The diabetes medication Dr. Kowalski prescribed is $547?" Her voice trembled. "I can't afford that. My Medicare has a gap, and I'm already stretching to cover my other medications."

Marcus knew exactly which medication she'd been prescribed. His company's newest diabetes drug—the one he'd convinced Dr. Kowalski to prescribe instead of the $42 monthly generic. They performed nearly identically in clinical trials.

Mrs. Patterson left without filling the prescription.

Marcus sat frozen. He'd spent twenty minutes that morning explaining to Dr. Kowalski why the expensive option was "better"—emphasizing minor differences while downplaying the 1,200% cost increase.

That evening, Marcus couldn't eat dinner. Couldn't look at his kids. Couldn't sleep.

He'd been Mrs. Patterson dozens of times. Hundreds, probably. He'd convinced doctors to prescribe expensive medications to vulnerable people who couldn't afford them—all so he could hit sales targets and earn bonuses.

The Decision

Over the next month, Marcus did what he'd been avoiding for years. He read clinical studies comparing his company's expensive drugs to generic alternatives. He analyzed patient outcome data.

The conclusion was unavoidable: he'd been harming vulnerable people to earn commission.

Marcus faced an impossible choice. His family depended on his income. Jennifer had been out of the workforce for eleven years. They had a mortgage, two car payments, private school tuition. His salary supported their entire lifestyle.

Quitting meant financial catastrophe.

Staying meant continuing to harm people like Mrs. Patterson.

He sat with Jennifer in their living room late one Thursday night. "I can't do this anymore. I need to leave pharmaceutical sales."

Jennifer was quiet for a long time. Then: "We'll figure it out. I'd rather struggle financially than watch you lose yourself."

Marcus gave his notice three days later.

The Aftermath

The first six months were brutal. Marcus took a position selling medical devices—ethical products, honest pricing—earning $69,000. They lost $35,000 in annual income overnight.

Jennifer took a part-time job. They pulled their kids from private school. They sold one car. They canceled the vacation budget and cut entertainment spending.

Daily, Marcus questioned his decision. Had he ruined his family's financial stability?

He would wake in the middle of the night in a panic, calculating bills, questioning everything.

But something fundamental had shifted. The ulcer symptoms disappeared. He could look at himself in the mirror without avoiding his own eyes. He came home energized rather than drained.

His kids noticed. One evening, his daughter said, "Dad, you smile more now than you used to."

Jennifer observed the same thing. "Even though we have less money, we fight about money less. You're not stressed all the time. You're present with us again."

Two Years Later

Twenty-four months after Marcus left pharmaceutical sales, his total compensation had climbed to $82,000. Combined with Jennifer's part-time income, they were earning $92,800—approaching their previous income.

More importantly, their spending had adjusted. They'd discovered they didn't need the vacation budget—camping trips created better memories. The kids thrived with fewer activities and more family time.

But the real restoration wasn't financial. It was relational and spiritual.

Marcus's relationship with Jennifer had deepened. Walking

through financial difficulty together had created intimacy that prosperity never had.

His kids had watched their father sacrifice financially for his convictions. They'd seen integrity in action. His daughter told him she wanted to be a doctor who helped people who couldn't afford care. His son said he wanted a job where he could "help people like Dad does."

Marcus's spiritual life had come alive. Following Jesus had moved from Sunday routine to daily reality. The cost of discipleship wasn't theoretical—it was his $35,000 pay cut. And he'd discovered that Jesus' promise was true: the rewards far exceeded the sacrifice.

Today, Marcus mentors young professionals facing similar dilemmas. His advice: "Count the cost honestly. Following Jesus will cost you something real. But also count the cost of NOT following Him. What's it costing your soul to compromise daily?"

"For me, the math was clear once I asked the right question. It wasn't 'Can I afford to leave?' It was 'Can I afford to stay?'"

"Jesus asked what it profits someone to gain the whole world but lose their soul. I was on track to gain a comfortable income and lose myself. I chose differently. And I've never regretted it."

Linda's Social Transformation

Linda had built her entire social life around nightclub culture—weekend parties, concerts, bars, festivals. Her friend group of fifteen years centered around shared entertainment.

When Linda committed to following Jesus seriously at age 29, everything changed. She stopped going to clubs. She started attending Bible study instead of parties. She chose church over concerts.

The tension became unbearable. Linda made a decision that terrified her: She'd fully commit to following Jesus, even if it meant losing her social circle.

Three months after Linda stopped attending Friday night gatherings, her closest friend Megan texted: "We need to talk."

They met for coffee. Megan didn't waste time: "Linda, what's happened to you? You've become so religious. You've abandoned your friends. You act like you're better than us now."

Linda had been dreading this conversation. "I'm not better than anyone. I'm just trying to live differently."

"Differently? You've completely changed. You don't go out anymore. You're always at church or Bible study. We've been friends for twelve years, Linda. And now you can't even come to my birthday party because it's at a bar?"

Linda felt tears forming. "It's not about judging you. It's about... I can't live that way anymore. The clubbing, the drinking—it was making me empty. I was pretending to be happy, but I was miserable."

"So now you've found Jesus, so we're not good enough for you."

Linda's tears spilled over. "That's not fair. I still love you. I still want to be friends. But I can't do the club scene anymore. Can't our friendship exist outside of bars?"

Megan stood up. "I don't know, Linda. The person sitting here isn't the friend I knew."

She left. Linda sat at that coffee shop for another hour, crying, questioning everything.

The Lonely Season

Four weeks later, Linda experienced her loneliest morning as a believer.

It was Saturday—10 AM. In her old life, her phone would be buzzing with group chat messages, Instagram tags, plans forming.

This Saturday, her phone was silent.

No texts. No invitations. No plans.

Her old friend group had moved on without her. The group chat she'd been part of for five years—she'd been removed from at some point.

Linda sat on her couch, looking at her silent phone, and felt crushingly alone. She'd chosen Jesus, and the cost was every friendship she'd built over twelve years.

Was it worth it?

Her Bible sat on the coffee table. She opened it and her eyes landed on Luke 14:26: "If anyone comes to me and does not hate father and mother, wife and children, brothers and sisters —yes, even their own life—such a person cannot be my disciple."

Linda knew Jesus didn't mean literal hate. He meant: Following Him must come first. Even before relationships you value most. Even when it costs you everything.

She closed the Bible, curled up on her couch, and cried. Following Jesus was supposed to bring abundant life. Right now, it felt like isolation and loss.

Finding New Community

The shift didn't happen overnight. Linda spent two months attending church and Bible study while feeling like an outsider.

But slowly, connections formed.

A woman named Denise invited Linda to coffee after Bible study. They talked for two hours—not about clubs or parties, but about faith struggles, family challenges, career questions. Linda left feeling seen in a way she hadn't experienced in years.

Denise invited Linda to a women's gathering at her house. Linda shared her story about losing her friend group. Three other women shared similar experiences. Linda realized she wasn't alone.

Two women, Rachel and Emma, started texting Linda regularly. They invited her to a Saturday morning hiking group. Seven women met weekly to hike and talk. Linda discovered she actually enjoyed mornings more than late nights.

Six months after leaving her old friend group, Linda had built a new community. Not the same kind of friendships—these weren't built around shared entertainment. They were built around shared values, mutual encouragement, spiritual growth.

The new friendships felt different. Deeper. More authentic. Less performance, more vulnerability. Less about impressing each other, more about supporting each other.

One Year Later

Thirteen months after her confrontation with Megan, Linda ran into her at a grocery store.

"You look... good. Happy," Megan said.

"I am happy."

"I thought you'd be miserable without your social life."

Linda smiled. "I thought I would be too. But I'm not. I have a different social life now. Different friends. It's actually better."

Megan looked skeptical. "Better than us?"

"Not better people. Better for me. Healthier. More real."

Megan paused. "I've been thinking about what you said. About pretending to be happy but being miserable. I... I think I've been pretending too."

Linda felt her heart soften. "Do you want to grab coffee sometime? Not to argue. Just to talk?"

"Yeah. I'd like that."

Two weeks later, Megan texted. They met for coffee. Megan asked questions about Linda's faith, her new community, why she'd made such a radical change.

"Was it worth it?" Megan asked. "Losing all of us?"

Linda thought carefully. "I didn't want to lose you. That hurt more than I can explain. But yes—following Jesus has been worth everything I gave up. And I'm hoping I haven't lost you permanently."

Six months later, Megan started attending church with Linda. Two years later, she gave her life to Christ. The friendship Linda thought she'd lost became deeper and more meaningful through the journey of faith.

The Promise That Endures

Jesus doesn't promise following Him will be easy or immediately rewarding in ways the world values. But He does promise it will be worth it.

> "In this world you will have trouble. But take heart! I have overcome the world" (John 16:33).

The troubles are real. The victory is greater.

Paul, who suffered extensively for following Jesus, declared:

> "I consider that our present sufferings are not worth comparing with the glory that will be revealed in us" (Rom. 8:18).

Present sacrifice. Future glory. Eternal perspective changes everything.

Marcus gave up $35,000 annually and gained peace, integrity, and restored relationships. Linda lost twelve years of friendships and gained authentic community and eventually led her best friend to Christ. Both discovered that Jesus' promise was true: the rewards far exceeded the sacrifice.

Your midnight doubts are normal. Your questions are legitimate. But remember: the same Jesus who died for you is alive today, working in ways you cannot see, preparing rewards you cannot imagine, and loving you more than you can comprehend.

The cost is real. The reward is greater. He's worth it. He's worth everything.

Questions for Your Heart

1. What specific aspect of following Jesus has cost you the most?
2. What benefits from following Jesus have you experienced that money cannot buy?
3. What would you lose if you stopped following Jesus that you cannot afford to lose?
4. When you honestly compare the eternal rewards with the temporal costs, which side weighs heavier?

Prayer

Jesus, I confess that sometimes I question whether following You is worth the cost. The sacrifices feel real while the rewards sometimes feel distant.

Help me see clearly what You've given me, not just what I've given up for You. Open my eyes to the peace, purpose, and hope that come from knowing You personally.

When the cost feels overwhelming, remind me of the greater cost of not following You. Help me trust that Your rewards—both now and eternally—exceed any sacrifice You ask me to make.

Give me faith to believe Your promises even when I can't see immediate benefits. Thank You for being worth whatever it costs to follow You. Strengthen my commitment during seasons of doubt.

In Your name, Amen.

Key Takeaway

Following Jesus costs everything but provides rewards that money cannot purchase—peace that sustains through crisis, purpose that transcends circumstances, relationships built on truth rather than performance, and eternal significance that outlasts every temporary pleasure.

Part II Summary

When God Speaks About YOUR Needs

You came to Part II carrying anxiety and impossible math. You leave with peace about *your* bills—not because circumstances suddenly changed, but because you learned to hear God's voice making specific promises about *your* household. And you discovered that His promises remain reliable even when your calculations do not.

What You Discovered About House

When your math failed, prayer moved heaven.
When your earthly provider was gone, your Maker became your Husband.
When employers broke promises, God blessed the work of your hands anyway.
When small gifts felt inadequate, God multiplied them beyond your ability to calculate.
When your treasure revealed your heart, you chose eternal significance over temporary comfort.
And when you counted the cost of following Jesus, you discovered He is worth everything.

Through six crisis-tested chapters, you learned a deeper kind of self-care—trusting God's promises for your needs instead of panicking over your circumstances.

Why This Matters

You cannot bless others from empty hands.
God filled *your* house so you could give from overflow rather than scarcity.
The widow who gave her final meal to the prophet received provision for her household for three years.
The widow who poured from a single jar of oil paid her debts and lived on the overflow.
These were not merely inspiring stories. They were blueprints —proof that God's voice concerning *your* provision is trustworthy.

The Bridge to Nations

Heaven positioned your heart to hear God's voice through worship.
House filled your hands by teaching you to trust His provision for your needs.
Now **Nations** awaits—learning to hear God's voice directing you to bless others from your overflow.

The House phase answered this question:
Will I trust God's provision for my household?

The Nations phase asks another:
Who is God directing me to bless with what He has placed in my hands—and will I obey when I hear His voice?

The progression continues: **Heaven → House → Nations.**

Your house is filled.

The same God who provided for your household when the math seemed impossible now desires to use your story to bless someone else's.

Ready?

Part III

Nations

Hearing God Direct You to Bless Others

Nicole checked her bank account and blinked at the balance. For the first time in three years, she had margin. Not wealth—just $180 after all bills were paid. But it was real overflow.

During her morning prayer, a thought wouldn't leave her mind: *Gloria from church—the single mom who mentioned struggling with childcare costs.*

Nicole knew Gloria earned $2,400 monthly. Childcare cost $1,800. The math didn't work.

"Use YOUR overflow to help with HER need," Nicole sensed God saying.

She hesitated. $180 wasn't much. It wouldn't solve Gloria's childcare problem long-term. But the prompting wouldn't leave.

That Sunday, Nicole handed Gloria an envelope with $180. "I know this doesn't cover everything, but I felt like God wanted me to help."

Gloria's eyes filled with tears. "This covers exactly one week of childcare. Which means I can work next week instead of missing shifts. Which means I keep my job."

Nicole didn't know it then, but her $180 would keep Gloria employed through a critical month. Gloria would get promoted six months later. The promotion would create margin in Gloria's budget—margin she'd use to help another struggling mom at church, who would help an elderly neighbor, creating a ripple of provision through their entire community.

All because Nicole heard God say, "Bless her with what I gave you."

From YOUR House to THEIR Breakthrough

Part I taught you to worship God with your finances. Part II taught you to trust His provision for YOUR household. Part III teaches you to hear God directing you toward others.

Once you've learned to love God with your wallet and trust His promises for YOUR needs, the natural overflow is loving your neighbor from the abundance He creates.

This isn't about having wealth. It's about having a willing heart that hears God say, "Bless them with what I gave you."

The Question Part III Answers

Who is God prompting YOU to bless with YOUR overflow—and will you obey when you hear His voice?

The chapters ahead show how small obedience creates impact beyond what you can see: lunches that feed thousands, legacies that bless generations, everyday generosity that multiplies in ways only God orchestrates.

Listen. He's speaking.

Chapter 15

The Macedonian Privilege

Paul had a problem. The Corinthian church was wealthy, educated, influential—but their giving had stalled. They'd started a collection for Jerusalem believers a year earlier with enthusiasm and big promises. A year later? The momentum had died.

Meanwhile, another group of churches—poor, persecuted, afflicted—was giving with extraordinary generosity.

So Paul held up a mirror:

> "Moreover, brethren, we make known to you the grace of God bestowed on the churches of Macedonia: that in a great trial of affliction, the abundance of their joy and their deep poverty abounded in the riches of their liberality. For I bear witness that according to their ability, yes, and beyond their ability, they were freely willing, imploring us with much urgency that we would receive the gift and the fellowship of the ministering to the saints" (2 Cor. 8:1-4).

Read that slowly. Let the contrasts sink in.

Great trial of affliction.
Deep poverty.

Yet somehow—

Abundance of joy.
Riches of their liberality.
Beyond their ability.
Freely willing.
Much urgency.

How does deep poverty produce rich generosity? How does affliction create abundant joy? How do you give beyond your ability when you're already lacking? How do you beg people to let you give when most in crisis beg to receive?

Paul's answer: "the grace of God bestowed on the churches of Macedonia."

The grace of God. In ancient Hebrew understanding, the word for grace—*chen*—is pictured as a seed protected by a fence. God's Word, His promises planted in hearts, preserved by Him despite circumstances that try to uproot them.

The Macedonians weren't superhuman. They weren't wealthier than they appeared. They were genuinely poor, genuinely afflicted, genuinely facing trials that justified self-protection.

But God, by His grace, kept His Word alive in their hearts. His promises about provision, His truth about His character, His voice calling them to generous worship—all stayed rooted. Their circumstances couldn't uproot what He'd planted.

And from that protected truth came behavior that defied natural explanation: cheerful giving from deep poverty, abundant joy in affliction, begging for the privilege to give beyond ability.

Two Sources, Two Outcomes

Your financial behavior flows from whatever source dominates your heart.

If circumstances dominate:

You give sparingly because you're calculating survival. You hold back because fear is louder than faith. You measure every dollar against worst-case scenarios. You hear "give" and think about loss, risk, danger. Even when you give, it's grudging—complying with obligation while resenting the cost.

If God's voice dominates:

You give generously because His promises are louder than your panic. You release resources because His voice is clearer than your fear. You measure decisions against His faithfulness, not just your bank balance. You hear "give" and think about partnership with God, opportunity to trust Him, invitation to watch Him prove faithful. When you give, it's cheerful—flowing from genuine trust.

Paul says it explicitly:

> "Each of you should give what you have decided in your heart to give, not reluctantly or under compulsion, for God loves a cheerful giver" (2 Cor. 9:7).

Not reluctantly—that's giving while circumstances dominate.

Not under compulsion—that's giving from obligation you resent.

But cheerfully—that's giving when God has preserved His Word in your heart so deeply that His promises feel more real than your poverty.

The Macedonians weren't denying circumstances. Paul doesn't say they faced "minor challenges." He says *great trial of affliction* and *deep poverty*. They knew exactly what they were facing.

But God, by His grace, preserved what He'd spoken. And from that truth came behavior that looked insane by natural calculation but made perfect sense from a kingdom perspective.

The Generosity That Flows vs. The Obligation That Grudges

Paul tells the Corinthians to prepare their gift

> "as a matter of generosity and not as a grudging obligation" (2 Cor. 9:5).

Both groups are giving. Both are handing over money. But the source is completely different.

Grudging obligation says: "I have to do this. The church expects it. I'll comply, but I'll resent every dollar. My heart will calculate what this costs me—what I could have done with this money, what I'm giving up, how this puts me at risk."

That's giving while circumstances dominate. Fear of scarcity is louder than faith in God's provision.

Generous flow says: "I get to do this. God is inviting me to participate. I've heard His voice, and I trust His promises. My heart celebrates what this represents—partnership with God, obedience to His direction, opportunity to watch Him prove faithful."

That's giving when God has done His work. His Word about provision is more real than panic about scarcity.

The Macedonians didn't give grudgingly. Paul says they were "freely willing"—it flowed from genuine desire, not manufactured duty. They gave "beyond their ability" because God had so thoroughly preserved His truth in their hearts that they actually *wanted* to give more than logic said they should.

They were "imploring us with much urgency" to let them participate. Begging. Pleading. Insisting.

Most people in financial crisis beg to receive. The Macedonians begged to give.

That's God acting by His grace—preserving His Word from circumstances that would otherwise produce fear-based decisions.

When Your Math Doesn't Add Up

Daniel stared at the medical bill. $3,800. His HSA had $1,200. His emergency fund—already depleted from last month's car repair—had maybe $300 left.

The bill was due in thirty days. His next paycheck would barely cover rent and groceries.

He'd already given his tithe two weeks ago—that wasn't the question. The tithe belonged to the Lord. But now, during morning quiet time, God had been speaking to him about something else.

An offering. Above the tithe.

Three weeks earlier, his church announced a Jubilee Campaign—partnering with an organization that forgives medical debt. For every dollar donated, $100 in debt is eliminated. The vision: erase $5 million in medical debt for 500 families.

Daniel had sat in that service, staring at faces carrying bills identical to his own. Families crushed under debt from surgeries, cancer treatment, and chronic conditions. He knew exactly what they felt—the 3 AM panic, the impossible math.

During his quiet time, he'd been reading 2 Corinthians 8—the Macedonians giving from deep poverty. Then Deuteronomy 15:10:

> "Give generously... then because of this the LORD your God will bless you in all your work and in everything you put your hand to."

He'd sensed God speaking: "Daniel, I'll provide for your household. Trust Me with an offering. I know about your $3,800 bill. Give so others can be freed."

Daniel knew what his circumstances were screaming: *You*

can't afford an offering. Your medical bills come first. Wait until you're stable.

The voice was loud. Logical. Compelling.

But God's promise felt more real than the bill on his table.

Daniel opened his banking app. He'd been thinking $100. But another number came: $500.

Five hundred dollars. When he had a $2,300 shortfall and an empty emergency fund.

His $500 would eliminate $50,000 in medical debt—maybe five families could breathe again.

Daniel transferred the money.

Not grudgingly. But with what surprised him: a sense of release. Of giving others the freedom he was trusting God to give him.

The math still didn't work. The bill was still due. The emergency fund was still empty.

But fear had lost its grip.

Two weeks later, his employer announced surprise bonuses. Daniel's share: $4,100.

The bill got paid. The emergency fund got replenished. Money left over.

Daniel discovered what the Macedonians learned: When you trust God's promise about provision, giving stops feeling like sacrifice and starts feeling like partnership.

He'd given from his crisis. God multiplied it into others' freedom.

Two Questions to Examine Your Heart

Paul's contrast between "generosity" and "grudging obligation" forces honest examination:

Question 1: When you give, what's happening in your heart?

Are you calculating loss? Resenting the cost? Wishing you didn't have to? Feeling anxious about what this leaves you with?

That's grudging obligation. Circumstances dominating.

Or are you sensing partnership with God? Trusting His promises? Responding to His voice? Experiencing peace that doesn't match the math?

That's generous flow. God has preserved what He spoke.

Question 2: What would it take for you to give cheerfully from crisis?

The Macedonians gave from deep poverty. Daniel gave with a medical bill looming. Both experienced the same thing: God preserving His Word so thoroughly that His promises felt more real than their panic.

What would it take for that to be true in your life?

Not what would it take for circumstances to improve so giving feels safe. But what would it take for God to so thoroughly preserve His Word in your heart that you could give cheerfully even when circumstances scream otherwise?

That's the journey this book is inviting you into.

The Privilege You're Being Offered

Paul calls this a privilege.

Not a burden. Not an obligation. A privilege.

> "They were freely willing, imploring us with much urgency that we would receive the gift and the fellowship of the ministering to the saints" (2 Cor. 8:4).

The Macedonians saw participation in God's work—even from poverty—as a privilege worth begging for.

Why? Because God had so thoroughly preserved His truth in their hearts that they saw what natural eyes can't see: Giving isn't primarily about money leaving your account. It's about relationship with God that the money represents.

Hearing His voice and responding.

Trusting His promises despite circumstances.

Choosing which source will dominate behavior.

Discovering He's faithful even when math says He can't be.

The Macedonians experienced it. Daniel experienced it. You can experience it.

Not by denying circumstances. But by letting God preserve what He's spoken—so His promises stay rooted even when storms try to uproot them.

What Voice Controls Your Wallet?

When financial pressure comes—and it will—which voice controls your wallet?

Circumstances screaming about survival, demanding self-protection?

Or God whispering promises about provision, inviting generous partnership?

The Macedonians faced that choice. Deep poverty. Great affliction. But they'd learned to recognize God's voice. So they gave. Cheerfully. Abundantly. Beyond their ability.

Daniel faced that choice. Medical bills. Empty emergency fund. But he'd heard God during prayer. So he gave. An offering. Above the tithe. Despite the crisis.

Now you face that choice.

Different crisis. Different numbers. Same fundamental decision: Which voice will control your wallet?

What if the financial pressure you're facing isn't primarily about money—but about learning to hear God's voice clearly enough that His promises become more real than your panic?

What if this crisis is actually an invitation to experience what the Macedonians experienced: the abundance of joy that comes from trusting God's voice even when your math says you can't afford to?

He's inviting you.

The question is: Will you respond?

Questions for Your Heart

1. When financial pressure hits, which voice gets louder —God's promises or your circumstances? What would help you hear Him more clearly?
2. Think about your last several gifts. Were they "generous flow" or "grudging obligation"? What does your honest answer reveal about which source dominates your heart?
3. The Macedonians begged for the privilege to give from deep poverty. What would need to shift in your heart for giving to feel like privilege rather than burden?
4. If God asked you to give an offering tomorrow despite your current financial pressure, what would you say to Him? What does that conversation reveal?

Prayer

God, I want what the Macedonians had. Not their poverty—but their joy. Not their affliction—but their trust.

Teach me to hear Your voice about my finances clearly enough that Your promises become more real than my panic. Preserve Your Word in my heart. Keep it rooted when circumstances try to uproot it.

I don't want to give grudgingly from obligation. I want to give cheerfully from trust. I don't want circumstances controlling my wallet. I want Your voice directing my generosity.

Show me what it means to give beyond my ability, like they did. Not recklessly. Not foolishly. But with confident trust that You'll provide even when my math says You can't.

Make this crisis an opportunity to discover Your faithfulness. Let me experience what they experienced: that when You preserve Your Word in my heart, provision flows from a source my circumstances can't touch.

In Jesus' name, amen.

Key Takeaway

When God, by His grace, preserves His Word in your heart, His promises become stronger than your circumstances—and you can give cheerfully from deep poverty because the source of your provision isn't your bank account, it's His faithfulness.

Chapter 16

Sowing and Reaping

When Your Overflow Blesses Nations

The invitation card sat on our dining room table for two weeks. "Kingdom Builders Missions Banquet - October."

My wife and I had walked past it dozens of times. We'd talked about going. I thought about what it might cost us if we did go.

Then our daughter called. She works at the church and had been helping organize the event. "Are you planning to come to the banquet?" she asked.

Something in her voice—or maybe something in our hearts—made this feel like more than a casual question. This felt like God's voice breaking through our comfortable patterns.

The Principle That Governs Kingdom Giving

> "The point is this: whoever sows sparingly will also reap sparingly, and whoever sows generously will also reap generously. Each one must give as he has decided in his heart, not reluctantly or under compulsion, for God loves a cheerful giver. And God is able to make all grace abound to you, so that having all sufficiency in all things at all times, you

> may abound in every good work" (2 Cor. 9:6-8).

Paul reveals a spiritual law as reliable as gravity: You reap what you sow. Not just in quantity, but in quality. Sparingly or generously. Reluctantly or cheerfully.

But notice what follows: God makes grace abound so that you may abound in every good work. The provision isn't the goal—it's the means. God provides for YOUR house so you can bless THEIR needs.

From Orphan Thinking to Royal Generosity

For years, my wife and I had given what we "could afford"—carefully calculated amounts that wouldn't disrupt our security.

We'd learned to hear His voice calling us to worship Him with our finances. We'd learned to trust His promises for OUR household, to believe His Word about OUR specific needs.

But we were learning something else: Since we don't have to focus totally on our own survival anymore, we can turn with vision to how we can be generous on every occasion to others.

That shift—from survival mode to generous vision—is what the Kingdom Builders banquet was about to activate.

Rachel's Online Course: Building a Net

Before I share our Kingdom Builders story, let me show you how one teacher discovered that God sometimes directs you to build infrastructure that captures ongoing provision for ongoing generosity.

Rachel taught high school English for eleven years on a teacher's salary of $52,000 annually. During summer break, she often tutored students privately to supplement her income.

One afternoon while explaining essay structure to a struggling student, an idea hit her: What if she created a video course teaching essay writing skills that students could access anytime?

She pushed the thought aside. She wasn't a tech person. Who would buy a course when students could just Google essay tips?

But the idea wouldn't leave. For three weeks that summer, Rachel kept reading about multiplication during her devotions—the talents parable, the widow's oil, Peter's net-breaking catch.

One morning, she sensed God saying clearly: "You've been given knowledge. Build a net that captures ongoing provision, then use that provision to bless students who can't afford help."

The phrase "build a net" stuck with her. Not a one-time payment for tutoring one student. A net—something that would catch provision repeatedly, creating ongoing income that could fund ongoing generosity.

Rachel spent her summer break creating "Essay Excellence: From Struggling to Strong in 30 Days." She invested $480 in equipment and hosting, plus 120 hours of work.

Her husband thought she was wasting her summer. "You could be tutoring and actually making money."

But Rachel had heard God's voice clearly.

First month: three purchases. Revenue: $141.

She'd invested an entire summer to earn $141. She could have tutored and earned $3,000 in that same time.

But she kept promoting it. By December, she'd sold twenty-seven courses. Revenue: $1,269. After expenses, she netted about $1,000.

More importantly, students were getting results. Parents emailed thanking her. Teachers recommended it to their students. The course was working.

Year two changed everything. Word-of-mouth spread. Parents told other parents. Teachers recommended it to struggling students. Homeschool groups discovered it.

Rachel sold ninety-three courses in eight months. Revenue: $4,371.

She realized she'd actually built a net. The course existed now—complete, available 24/7. She wasn't trading hours for dollars. Each sale was like a fish caught in a net—provision captured through infrastructure she'd built once but could use repeatedly.

Then Rachel heard God's voice again: "Now give it away."

She started offering free course codes to students whose families couldn't afford the $47 price. Teachers at underfunded schools could request codes for struggling students. Families experiencing financial hardship could apply.

Year three: Rachel gave away 197 free course codes while selling 847 total courses. Revenue: $39,809. Free courses given: nearly $9,300 value.

A teacher in an underfunded Philadelphia school used the free codes with her entire class of twenty-nine students. Test scores improved dramatically. Three other teachers at that school started using it.

A student experiencing homelessness used a free code to improve her college application essays. She received a full scholarship. She wrote Rachel: "Your course didn't just teach me to write. It gave me hope that someone cared about my success even though I couldn't afford to pay for help."

Rachel had built a net that captured provision repeatedly. Then she used that ongoing provision to fund ongoing generosity—giving away nearly 200 courses to students who couldn't afford help.

The Night Our Giving Changed

The Kingdom Builders banquet was beautiful. Worship music played softly. Missionaries shared stories of transformation around the world.

Then the visiting pastor opened his Bible to 2 Corinthians 9:

> "And God is able to make all grace abound to you, so that having all sufficiency in all things at all times, you may abound in every good work... You will be enriched in every way so

> that you can be generous on every occasion"
> (2 Cor. 9:8, 11).

That phrase intrigued me: "so that you can be generous on every occasion."

Not "so that you can be comfortable." Not "so that you can save for retirement."

So that you can be generous. On every occasion.

The presentation continued. Missionaries planting churches in unreached regions. Homes being built for families with nothing. Children rescued from trafficking. Communities transformed through education and the Gospel.

I was moved. My wife was moved.

But we'd been here before. Moved by great causes. Moved to give—comfortably. We had a pattern: calculate what we could afford without disrupting our plans, give that amount, feel good about ourselves.

But that phrase wouldn't leave me: "generous on every occasion."

I leaned over to my wife. "What if we broke through our comfortable pattern?"

She looked at me. I saw the same wrestling in her eyes that I felt in my gut.

We'd failed at pledges before. Years ago, we'd committed to giving amounts we couldn't sustain. The failure had taught us to be "realistic," to give only what we were sure we could manage.

But was "realistic" the same as "generous"?

The Breakthrough Moment

The pastor was explaining the sowing and reaping principle. "When you sow sparingly—giving only what's comfortable, what doesn't cost you anything—you reap sparingly. But when you sow generously—giving what requires faith, what stretches you beyond your comfort—you reap generously. Not just in money. In capacity. In vision. In partnership with God."

That word hit me: capacity.

What if God wanted to enlarge our capacity to give? What if we'd been sowing sparingly—comfortable amounts that required no faith—and wondering why we weren't experiencing breakthrough?

My wife and I had been praying for breakthrough in our finances, asking God to expand our vision for making a difference and legacy impact.

What if this banquet was God answering that prayer—but requiring us to sow at a level that actually required faith?

The $10,000 Question

The commitment cards were distributed. People around us were filling them out quietly, privately.

I looked at the card. Various amounts listed. Monthly options. Annual options.

My wife and I hadn't discussed any specific giving plans on

the drive over. We'd assumed we'd give something comfortable, manageable, within our predictable pattern.

But now, sitting there with that phrase echoing—"generous on every occasion"—I felt God asking: Are you ready to break through comfortable into generous?

I wrote a number on the card: $10,000.

I showed my wife. Her eyes widened. That wasn't what we'd discussed. That wasn't comfortable. That wasn't what we "could afford" without adjusting other plans.

"Are you sure?" she whispered.

I wasn't sure. But I was tired of sowing sparingly. Tired of giving from comfort instead of faith. Tired of asking God to enlarge our capacity while refusing to step into situations that would require enlarged capacity.

"I think this is what 'generous' looks like," I whispered back. "Not comfortable. Generous."

Unknowingly, this was the exact number she'd received from God—the "scary" amount that would profane the comfortable old pattern.

She held my gaze for a long moment. Then she nodded. "Let's do it."

We filled out the card together. $10,000. Not to Kingdom Builders—to the Kingdom. To missionaries we'd never meet. To children we'd never see. To churches that would be planted in nations we'd never visit.

From our house, to their breakthrough.

What Happened After We Sowed Generously

I won't tell you that $10,000 immediately appeared in our bank account. This isn't a formula: give big → get bigger.

But something did happen.

Our capacity to give enlarged. After committing to $10,000, other giving opportunities didn't intimidate us the way they used to. We'd crossed a threshold. When you sow at one level, you develop capacity to sow at that level again.

Agreement with my wife became powerful. Making that decision together—wrestling together, deciding together, committing together—created a unity in our giving we'd never experienced. Now when opportunities arise, we're not fighting about them. We're partnering in them.

Our vision expanded. We started seeing needs we'd been blind to before. We started thinking about legacy and impact instead of just bills and security.

God provided for the commitment. Not through a windfall. Through increased income over the following months, through wisdom about expenses, through provision from sources we hadn't orchestrated. We're making the commitment without strain.

But here's what changed most: We learned what "so that you can be generous on every occasion" actually means.

It doesn't mean being wealthy. It means having capacity—enlarged capacity—to respond generously when God directs you. It means not being trapped in survival thinking even when circumstances are tight.

The Pattern Scripture Reveals

> "He who supplies seed to the sower and bread for food will supply and multiply your seed for sowing and increase the harvest of your righteousness. You will be enriched in every way so that you can be generous on every occasion, and through us your generosity will result in thanksgiving to God" (2 Cor. 9:10-11).

God supplies seed. He multiplies seed for sowing. You sow generously. He increases the harvest. Others give thanks to God.

YOUR overflow becoming seed that blesses others and creates worship to God.

The Heart Behind Generous Sowing

> "Each one must give as he has decided in his heart, not reluctantly or under compulsion, for God loves a cheerful giver" (2 Cor. 9:7).

God doesn't want reluctant givers. He doesn't want people giving under pressure. He wants cheerful givers who've decided in their hearts.

That's what happened to us at the Kingdom Builders banquet. We decided in our hearts. Not because we were pressured.

Not because we were manipulated. Because we'd heard God's voice throughout this entire journey: Worship Me with your finances. Trust Me to provide for YOUR household. Now bless THEM from YOUR overflow.

The $10,000 wasn't reluctant. It was decided. It was cheerful. Because we'd learned that God is faithful to His promises about provision for OUR house.

Your Invitation to Generous Sowing

You may never attend a Kingdom Builders banquet. You may never create an online course like Rachel. But you will face moments when God asks you to sow generously instead of sparingly.

Maybe it's a missions offering. Maybe it's a need in your community. Maybe it's a prompting to help a specific family. Maybe it's an opportunity to build a "net" that captures provision you can use to bless others repeatedly.

When that moment comes, remember the principle: whoever sows sparingly reaps sparingly. Whoever sows generously reaps generously.

Not as formula. As kingdom reality.

"So that you can be generous on every occasion."

Questions for Your Heart

1. Are you sowing sparingly (comfortable amounts requiring no faith) or generously (amounts that stretch your capacity)?

2. What would change if you believed God wants to enlarge your capacity to give, not just your bank account?
3. Who is God prompting you to bless generously from the overflow He's created in YOUR house?
4. What past failure with giving might be keeping you from breakthrough into generous sowing?
5. What "net" could you build—a skill, knowledge, or resource packaged in a way that creates ongoing provision you could use for ongoing generosity?

Prayer

Heavenly Father, thank You for providing for our household. Thank You for being faithful to Your promises about provision for our needs.

Enlarge our capacity to give. Expand our vision beyond survival to generous impact. Help us hear Your voice directing us toward specific opportunities to sow generously.

Forgive us for sowing sparingly—giving only what's comfortable; what doesn't cost us anything. Teach us to sow generously—giving what requires faith; what stretches us beyond our comfort.

Show us if You want us to build "nets"—infrastructure that captures provision repeatedly so we can give repeatedly. Give us wisdom to package our knowledge, skills, or resources in ways that create ongoing harvest for ongoing generosity.

Use our overflow to bless nations. Let our generosity create thanksgiving to You. Make us partners in Your work around the world.

We want to be generous on every occasion. Not reluctantly. Not under compulsion. But cheerfully, because we trust that You who supplied seed for our sowing will multiply our seed and increase the harvest.

From our house to their breakthrough. For Your glory.

In Jesus' name, Amen.

Key Takeaway

Whoever sows sparingly reaps sparingly; whoever sows generously reaps generously. God provides for YOUR house not just to meet YOUR needs, but to create overflow so you can be generous on every occasion—sometimes through building "nets" that capture provision repeatedly, allowing you to fund ongoing generosity from ongoing harvest.

Chapter 17
The Boy's Lunch Miracle

When YOUR Small Offering Feeds THEIR Hunger

Five thousand hungry men, plus women and children—fifteen thousand people total. No food vendors. No restaurants nearby. The day had stretched long, and stomachs were growling.

The disciples calculated the impossibility:

> "Send the crowds away so they can go to the surrounding countryside and villages and buy themselves something to eat" (Mark 6:36).

But a young boy had packed lunch that morning. Five small barley loaves—the bread of the poor. Two small fish—dried, probably salted. Enough for one person, embarrassingly inadequate for such massive need.

Andrew spotted the boy and brought him to Jesus, voicing what everyone was thinking:

> "Here is a boy with five small barley loaves and

> two small fish, but how far will they go among so many?" (John 6:9).

The boy didn't hesitate. When Jesus reached for his lunch, he simply released it. Everything he had for the day—gone. Given freely to feed a need far beyond anything his small gift could solve.

Jesus took those five loaves and two fish, gave thanks, and began distributing them. The miracle didn't happen all at once in His hands. It happened as the food moved through the crowd. Disciples kept breaking bread that somehow never ran out. Fish that multiplied as they passed from person to person.

Not only did everyone eat until satisfied, but

> "they gathered twelve basketfuls of broken pieces" (John 6:13).

One boy heard Jesus' silent call for provision and responded with everything he had. Fifteen thousand people ate their fill. Twelve baskets of leftovers remained—more than what they started with.

The Widow's Last Meal

Centuries earlier, another person faced the same impossible choice: give away your last food or keep it for yourself.

A widow in Zarephath stood during devastating famine, gathering sticks to prepare one final meal. She had exactly enough flour and oil left for herself and her son. After that—starvation.

Then the prophet Elijah appeared, requesting water and bread.

Her response revealed total desperation:

> "I don't have any bread—only a handful of flour in a jar and a little olive oil in a jug. I am gathering a few sticks to take home and make a meal for myself and my son, that we may eat it—and die" (1 Kings 17:12).

Elijah's reply contradicted every survival instinct:

> "Don't be afraid. Go home and do as you have said. But first make a small loaf of bread for me from what you have and bring it to me, and then make something for yourself and your son. For this is what the LORD, the God of Israel, says: 'The jar of flour will not be used up and the jug of oil will not run dry until the day the LORD sends rain on the land'" (1 Kings 17:13-14).

Give your last meal to feed someone else. Trust God for tomorrow's provision.

The widow heard God's voice through Elijah's words. She chose to believe what contradicted her circumstances. She obeyed despite her terror.

> "She went away and did as Elijah had told her. So there was food every day for Elijah and for the woman and her family. For the jar of flour was not used up and the jug of oil did not run dry, in keeping with the word of the LORD spoken by Elijah" (1 Kings 17:15-16).

One woman gave her last handful of flour. God created daily provision that sustained three people through years of famine. The multiplication never stopped as long as the need continued.

Angel's Crisis: When $200 Is All You Have

Angel had run "Angel's Kitchen," a Mexican food truck in downtown Phoenix, for three years. The first two years were profitable—she cleared about $2,800 monthly. But year three brought a decline. New competitors. A trendy restaurant district pulling customers. Construction closing her best spot.

By October, she was barely surviving. She needed $1,200 just to stay operational through November—commissary kitchen rent, truck maintenance, and personal bills.

She had $200 in her checking account.

Wednesday morning, October 23rd, she opened her Bible during what felt more like desperate bargaining than quiet time. "God, I need help. Show me what to do."

The passage from her reading plan: the feeding of five thousand. One phrase caught her attention:

> "You give them something to eat" (Mark 6:37).

You give them.

Angel thought about the homeless community in Margaret T. Hance Park, three blocks from her usual parking spot. Thirty to forty people gathered there daily. She drove past them every day, too focused on her own survival to think about theirs.

Now, with her Bible open and $200 in her account, she couldn't shake the thought: *Feed them first.*

"God, that's insane," she said out loud. "If I spend this $200 on food for homeless people, I'll have nothing. I'll lose the truck. I'll lose everything."

You give them something to eat.

The practical voice presented clear reasoning: "Use that $200 for brake work. Stay operational. Generate revenue."

But the quieter voice kept repeating: *Give them what you have. Trust Me for what you need.*

She thought about the widow with her last handful of flour. She thought about the boy with five loaves and two fish. Both gave everything they had. Both trusted God to handle what came next.

"Okay, God. I'll give first. You handle my bills."

Tuesday Evening in the Park

Angel ordered ingredients—quality food, not scraps. Flour tortillas, seasoned chicken, beef, rice, beans, fresh vegetables. Enough for forty complete meals. Total cost: $187.

Remaining balance: $13.

On Tuesday afternoon, she prepped in the commissary kitchen. Forty full-sized burritos, fresh pico de gallo, rice and beans as sides. She loaded her truck and drove to the park around 5:30 PM.

"It's free," she told the first cautious person. "Just take what you want."

A woman named Teresa approached, suspicious. "What's the catch?"

"No catch. I just felt like God wanted me to feed people today."

Teresa stared at her for a long time. "Thank you. I haven't eaten since yesterday morning."

Over two hours, Angel served thirty-nine people. Miguel, who'd lost his factory job. Jennifer, evicted after her husband died. Carlos, who worked full-time but couldn't afford Phoenix rent on $12 an hour.

By 7:30 PM, her truck was empty. Every burrito gone. Every side dish distributed.

She drove home with an empty truck and an empty bank account. Rent due in seven days. Commissary kitchen rent due in twelve.

She'd obeyed. Now what?

The Multiplication Nobody Expected

Wednesday and Thursday passed quietly. Friday afternoon, a woman approached her truck. "You're the one who fed people in the park Tuesday, right? My friend Teresa told me. I'm opening a small event planning business. Can you cater for my first client's party? Fifty people, next Saturday. $600."

Angel's hands shook while writing up the contract.

That Sunday after church, a man approached. "I heard about what you did on Tuesday. My company does quarterly team lunches. Would you be interested? Thirty people, four times a year."

Over four weeks, Angel signed contracts with three businesses for regular catering. Another company hired her for their annual holiday party—180 people. A wedding coordinator reached out.

By November's end, her daily revenue had increased from $250 to over $1,000 when counting catering contracts. By December, she'd cleared more in one month than the previous three combined.

But here's what mattered more than business success.

Every Tuesday evening, Angel drove to the park and gave away meals—ten percent of her weekly revenue. Not leftovers. Intentional, planned meals.

She fed Teresa every week. Miguel. Jennifer. Carlos. Others whose names she learned.

Teresa volunteered at a shelter because "someone showed me kindness when I needed it." Miguel got hired by a construction company and now mentors young men from prison. Jennifer found housing through a program Angel connected her to.

Six months later, a reporter featured Angel's Tuesday feeding program. A nonprofit leader read that story: "We help people transitioning out of homelessness. Can we partner with you for meals and job training?"

Within a year, Angel's food truck had become more than a business—it was a pathway. People came for food, learned about jobs, connected with resources, and found hope.

Angel hired three employees from the homeless community she'd been feeding. All three moved into stable housing within six months.

The Pattern Jesus Kept Repeating

Jesus didn't feed multitudes just once. Mark 8 records another feeding miracle—this time four thousand people with seven loaves and a few small fish.

Same impossible need. Different day. Smaller starting provision.

Jesus asked His disciples:

> "How many loaves do you have?" (Mark 8:5).

Seven loaves. A few fish. Totally inadequate for four thousand hungry people.

But Jesus took what they had, gave thanks, and began distributing.

> "The people ate and were satisfied. Afterward the disciples picked up seven basketfuls of broken pieces that were left over" (Mark 8:8).

Why does Scripture record two separate feeding miracles? Because this isn't a one-time anomaly—it's how God works. Small offerings given in faith. Massive multiplication that exceeds calculations. Leftovers proving God's abundance surpasses human need.

Five loaves fed fifteen thousand with twelve baskets left. Seven loaves fed four thousand with seven baskets left. The pattern holds: God multiplies what's released to Him.

The widow's flour and oil never ran out as long as the need continued. The boy's lunch fed thousands. Angel's $200 multiplied into sustainable business and ongoing generosity.

The common thread? Heard God's voice. Gave what they had. Trusted Him to multiply it.

Who Is Hungry in Your World?

God is speaking. Scripture that catches your attention right when someone's need becomes visible. Clear sense during prayer that He's directing you toward a specific person or situation. Peace about giving despite what it costs you. Conviction you can't shake about what He's asking you to do.

Maybe it's literal hunger—someone who needs groceries this week. Maybe it's hunger for hope—someone drowning in bills who needs to know God provides. Maybe it's hunger for dignity—someone who needs a job, a chance, an opportunity you can offer.

The question isn't whether God is speaking. The question is whether you're listening when He directs you to give.

Questions for Your Heart

1. What small offering is God prompting you to give that could feed their needs?
2. Who is God directing you to bless with what you have in your hands today—even if it seems inadequate for their hunger?
3. What would happen if you obeyed His voice about giving even when your math says you can't afford it?
4. Whose hunger could your lunch satisfy if you listened when God directed you toward them?

Prayer

God, show me who You want me to feed with what's in my hands. Help me hear Your voice directing my small offerings toward their big hunger. Give me the widow's courage to give my last meal, the boy's willingness to release everything without guarantees. Make my inadequate gift Your multiplication miracle for people whose names I may not even know. Let my obedience feed multitudes beyond what I can calculate or control. In Jesus' name, Amen.

Key Takeaway

Your small offering in God's hands becomes His abundant provision for their desperate need. Loving your neighbor means hearing God say, "feed them with your lunch" and obeying even when your gift seems embarrassingly inadequate—then watching Him multiply it into impact that feeds hunger far beyond what you could satisfy alone.

Chapter 18

Net-Breaking Abundance

Peter had fished all night and caught nothing. His nets were empty, his boat was clean, and his frustration was mounting. Professional fishermen don't fish in broad daylight—everyone knows fish bite at night.

Then Jesus said five words that changed everything:

> "Put out into deep water, and let down the nets for a catch" (Luke 5:4).

This contradicted everything Peter knew about fishing. But when God gives instructions that defy conventional wisdom, supernatural results follow obedience to His voice.

> "Master, we've worked hard all night and haven't caught anything. But because you say so, I will let down the nets" (Luke 5:5).

Peter's nets filled so quickly they began to tear. The catch was so enormous it nearly sank two boats. Professional fishermen became overwhelmed by abundance because they followed divine instructions instead of human reasoning.

> "When they had done so, they caught such a

> large number of fish that their nets began to break. So they signaled their partners in the other boat to come and help them, and they came and filled both boats so full that they began to sink" (Luke 5:6-7).

This wasn't provision for Peter's household alone. This was an overflow that blessed his business partners, created jobs for his crew, and impacted the entire fishing cooperative. One man's obedience to God's voice created breakthrough that required community participation to contain.

The Widow's Overflowing Oil

Centuries earlier, another widow experienced abundance that exceeded her capacity to manage alone.

A prophet's widow cried out to Elisha:

> "Your servant my husband is dead, and you know that he revered the LORD. But now his creditor is coming to take my two boys as his slaves" (2 Kings 4:1).

Elisha asked, "How can I help you? Tell me, what do you have in your house?"

> "Your servant has nothing there at all," she said, "except a small jar of olive oil" (2 Kings 4:2).

Nothing except a small jar of oil. Completely inadequate for her crisis.

Elisha's instructions seemed strange:

> "Go around and ask all your neighbors for empty jars. Don't ask for just a few. Then go inside and shut the door behind you and your sons. Pour oil into all the jars, and as each is filled, put it to one side" (2 Kings 4:3-4).

She obeyed. She borrowed containers from her neighbors—every jar, pot, and vessel they could spare. Then she began pouring from her one small jar.

The oil didn't stop flowing.

> "When all the jars were full, she said to her son, 'Bring me another one.' But he replied, 'There is not a jar left.' Then the oil stopped flowing. She went and told the man of God, and he said, 'Go, sell the oil and pay your debts. You and your sons can live on what is left'" (2 Kings 4:6-7).

One woman's obedience to pour out what seemed inadequate. Oil that multiplied beyond calculation. Provision that required her entire neighborhood's containers to hold. Debt paid. Sons rescued. Household sustained from the overflow.

The abundance exceeded her capacity to contain alone—it required community involvement.

The Pattern Scripture Reveals

> "One person gives freely, yet gains even more; another withholds unduly, but comes to poverty. A generous person will prosper; whoever refreshes others will be refreshed" (Prov. 11:24-25).

God's mathematics contradict human reasoning. Give freely—gain more. Withhold—come to poverty. Refresh others—be refreshed yourself.

The early church discovered this reality lived out in the community:

> "All the believers were together and had everything in common. They sold property and possessions to give to anyone who had need. And the Lord added to their number daily those who were being saved" (Acts 2:44-45, 47).

Individual obedience created community transformation. Personal generosity became a collective abundance. One person's overflow met another's need, and God multiplied the whole thing.

Bridget's Deep Water Call

Bridget had been catering for small events from her home kitchen for six years. Birthday parties. Baby showers. Small office luncheons. She earned about $45,000 annually—

enough to supplement her husband's income, but nothing dramatic.

During prayer one morning in March, Bridget sensed God saying something that made no sense: "Expand to corporate events."

Bridget's immediate response was logical resistance: "God, I don't have the equipment for large events. I've never catered for more than thirty people."

But the thought wouldn't leave. Corporate events. Expand. Launch out into deep water.

For three weeks, Bridget wrestled with this prompting. She researched commercial kitchen rentals—$1,200 monthly. She priced equipment—at least $8,000 for basics. She looked at corporate catering competitors—established companies with professional websites and full-time staff.

Everything logical said stay small, stay safe, stay in shallow water where she knew how to operate.

But the prompting intensified. Corporate events. Expand. Trust Me.

Bridget and her husband Dan sat at their kitchen table in April reviewing the numbers. To expand into corporate catering, they'd need about $15,000 in startup costs.

They had $3,200 in savings. They'd need to borrow $12,000 against their home equity.

"This is insane," Dan said quietly. "You're proposing we go into debt to expand a business that's working fine as is."

Bridget knew he was right from every logical perspective. "I know. But I can't shake the sense that God is directing me to do this. It feels like when Peter was told to launch into deep water—it doesn't make sense, but the instruction is clear."

Dan was quiet for a long time. Then: "If you genuinely believe God is directing this, then we have to obey. But I'm terrified."

"Me too."

They borrowed $12,000 from their house equity.

The First Contract: 800 People

Bridget rented commercial kitchen space and purchased equipment in May. She created a corporate catering menu. She built a simple website. She started reaching out to companies.

For six weeks, nothing happened. No calls. No inquiries. No contracts.

Bridget would stand in her rented commercial kitchen—$1,200 monthly whether she used it or not—and question everything. Had she misheard God?

July 12—ten weeks after launching—Bridget's phone rang.

"Hi, this is Shane from TechVision Solutions. We're hosting our annual conference August 15-16, about 800 attendees. We need catering for breakfast both days and lunch on the 15th. Can you handle that volume?"

Bridget's heart raced. Eight hundred people. This was exactly the deep water she'd been apprehensive of entering.

"Yes, we can absolutely handle that," Bridget heard herself say.

Her quote: $18,400.

They accepted.

Bridget worked eighteen-hour days preparing for that conference. The event went flawlessly. Shane pulled her aside afterward: "We have quarterly leadership meetings—about 100 people. Would you be interested in catering for those?"

Four quarterly meetings. Recurring revenue.

By February—six months after the TechVision conference—Bridget had secured eight companies with recurring contracts. Her revenue jumped from $45,000 annually to $285,000.

Six times her previous income.

But Bridget couldn't manage it alone anymore. The deep water was too deep for one person.

Hiring from the Margins

In March, Bridget faced a decision. She needed employees. She could hire experienced caterers—people who'd worked in restaurants and understood the industry.

Or she could do something different.

During prayer, Bridget felt God directing her: "Hire from the margins. Give opportunities to people others overlook."

Bridget started recruiting single moms from her church who needed flexible work. Women coming out of homelessness from a local ministry. Individuals rebuilding their lives after recovery.

She created a training program—teaching culinary skills, business practices, and customer service. She paid $18 hourly when competitors paid $12-$13. She offered flexible schedules that accommodated childcare needs.

It was inefficient initially. Training took time. Her profit margins were tighter.

But something remarkable happened.

Gloria was a single mom of three, working two minimum-wage jobs, barely surviving. Bridget hired her, trained her, gave her thirty hours weekly with schedule flexibility around her kids' school.

Within six months, Gloria's income increased enough that she could quit her second job. She was present for her kids' after-school activities for the first time in years. Two years later, Gloria became Bridget's kitchen manager, earning $52,000 annually—more than double what she'd earned working two jobs.

Gloria's eldest daughter, watching her mom's journey, decided to pursue culinary school. The blessing multiplied generationally.

Shanice was coming out of three years of homelessness and substance abuse recovery. No work history. No references. Bridget hired her for prep work. Eighteen months later, Shanice was running food prep teams, training new employees, and managing inventory. She'd saved enough for an apartment—her first stable housing in four years.

Shanice's story inspired the recovery ministry that had referred her. Four more women from that program joined Bridget's team.

Two years after Bridget launched into deep water, her business had become known for two things: excellent food and redemptive employment.

Churches and nonprofits started calling: "We hear you give people second chances. We have someone who needs an opportunity..."

Business clients chose Bridget specifically because her model aligned with their corporate values: "We want to work with companies that invest in their communities."

Bridget employed fifteen women—eight single mothers, four in recovery, three immigrants. Annual revenue: $480,000. But more importantly, fifteen households had moved from poverty to stability through dignified work.

The Nets-Breaking Moment

Year three brought Bridget's nets-breaking crisis. She had contracts worth $680,000 annually—more business than her team could handle.

She chose to launch a job training institute.

She partnered with her church and two nonprofits to create a formal culinary training program. Six-month curriculum. Paid internships. Job placement assistance.

The program enrolled twenty students year one. Eighteen graduated. Fifteen secured permanent employment.

Year two: thirty-five students. Year three: fifty students.

Bridget's obedience to launch into deep water had created an institution that blessed her entire community. Her nets hadn't just filled—they'd become a training system that multiplied impact exponentially.

When God's Instructions Contradict Your Expertise

Peter was an expert fisherman who knew deep water fishing at noon was foolish. The widow had one jar of oil—obviously inadequate for her debt. Bridget was an experienced caterer who knew expanding aggressively on borrowed money was risky.

But God's instructions aren't about your expertise. They're about positioning you for overflow that requires community involvement—blessing that's too big for you alone.

Peter's nets required his partners' boats. The widow's oil required her neighbors' containers. Bridget's business required hiring from the margins, which transformed households and inspired other businesses to follow her model.

Your Deep-Water Call

God might be calling you into deep water right now. It might sound illogical. It might contradict your expertise. It might require faith that terrifies you.

But remember: God doesn't call you into deep water to drown you. He calls you there to demonstrate His provision exceeds your expertise, to create blessings too big for you alone to manage, and to position you to bless your community systematically.

The question isn't whether you have the expertise for deep water. The question is whether you'll trust God's voice above your own reasoning.

Questions for Your Heart

1. What "deep water" instruction is God giving you that contradicts your conventional wisdom or expertise?
2. Where has He provided overflow in your life that requires community involvement to manage fully?
3. How might your current blessing be designed not just for your household but for systematic community impact?
4. Who are the "neighbors" God is directing you to involve in containing the abundance He's creating through your obedience?

Prayer

God, give me courage to obey Your voice when it contradicts my expertise. Help me trust that You're positioning me for abundance that exceeds my capacity—blessing that requires my community's involvement to contain.

Show me who needs to be involved in managing the overflow You're creating. Give me wisdom to hire, train, and empower people others overlook. Let my obedience create jobs, transform households, and inspire community-wide change.

When I'm petrified by deep water instructions, remind me of Peter's nets breaking with abundance, the widow's oil filling every borrowed jar, and Bridget's business becoming a training institute. You specialize in creating overflow that blesses entire communities through one person's obedience.

Position me for impact I can't orchestrate. Fill my nets until they require my neighbors' help to .contain. In Jesus' name, Amen.

Key Takeaway

When you follow God's voice into deep water despite conventional wisdom, He creates abundance that exceeds your capacity to manage alone—provision designed to bless your community systematically, requiring others' involvement to contain, transforming your obedience into their breakthrough.

Chapter 19

The Boaz Legacy

Boaz wasn't being randomly kind when he saw Ruth gleaning in his field. He was obeying a specific command God had spoken to Israel generations before:

> "If anyone is poor among your fellow Israelites in any of the towns of the land the LORD your God is giving you, do not be hardhearted or tightfisted toward them. Rather, be openhanded and freely lend them whatever they need" (Deut. 15:7-8).

God's voice through Scripture directed Boaz toward radical generosity. The Law required landowners to leave the edges of their fields unharvested so the poor could glean. But Boaz heard something more than legal obligation—he heard God's heart for the vulnerable, and he responded with openhanded abundance.

> "Do not be hardhearted or tightfisted toward them. Rather, be openhanded and freely lend them whatever they need... Give generously to them and do so without a grudging heart; then because of this the LORD your God will bless you in all your work and in everything

> you put your hand to. There will always be poor people in the land. Therefore I command you to be openhanded toward your fellow Israelites who are poor and needy in your land" (Deut. 15:7-8, 10-11).

Boaz understood this. When he instructed his workers to

> "let grain from the bundles fall purposely for her" (Ruth 2:16),

he was going beyond the minimum requirement. He heard God's heart for Ruth's household and responded with abundant provision. He left more than edges—he created overflow for her to gather.

The result? Ruth gathered an ephah of barley—about thirty pounds—in a single day. That's roughly two weeks' worth of food for her household from one day of gleaning. Boaz's obedience to God's voice about generosity didn't just help Ruth survive. It gave her dignity, provision, and hope.

And it positioned Boaz in God's eternal story.

Legacy Written in a Lineage

The book of Ruth ends with a genealogy that would have stunned ancient readers:

> "Boaz the father of Obed, Obed the father of Jesse, and Jesse the father of David" (Ruth 4:21-22).

The man who heard God's voice about generosity to a foreign widow became the great-grandfather of Israel's greatest king. His openhanded obedience placed him in the family tree of the Messiah. Matthew's gospel records it explicitly:

> "Boaz the father of Obed, whose mother was Ruth" (Matt. 1:5).

One decision to obey God's voice about leaving gleanings created a legacy that blessed the entire world.

The Good Samaritan: Who Is My Neighbor?

Centuries later, Jesus was asked directly: "Who is my neighbor?" He answered with a story about hearing God's voice and responding with openhanded generosity.

A man was attacked by robbers, stripped, beaten, and left half-dead on the roadside. A priest saw him and passed by on the other side. A Levite did the same. Both religious leaders heard nothing directing them toward the wounded man.

But a Samaritan—a despised outsider—saw him and heard something different.

> "When he saw him, he took pity on him. He went to him and bandaged his wounds, pouring on oil and wine. Then he put the man on his own donkey, brought him to an inn and took care of him. The next day he took out two denarii and gave them to the innkeeper. 'Look after him,' he said, 'and when I return, I

> will reimburse you for any extra expense you may have'" (Luke 10:33-35).

The Samaritan heard God's voice directing him toward a specific person in desperate need. He responded with immediate care, personal sacrifice, and ongoing provision. He didn't calculate the minimum requirement—he went beyond obligation to generous abundance.

Jesus concluded:

> "Go and do likewise" (Luke 10:37).

Love your neighbor. Hear God's voice directing you toward specific people in need. Respond with openhanded generosity that goes beyond minimum obligation.

The Pattern Scripture Reveals

Throughout Scripture, God honors those who hear His voice about generosity and respond in obedience.

Solomon wrote:

> "The generous will themselves be blessed, for they share their food with the poor" (Prov. 22:9).

> "Whoever is kind to the needy honors God" (Prov. 14:31).

In the book of Acts, Cornelius demonstrated this principle lived out:

> "He and all his family were devout and God-fearing; he gave generously to those in need and prayed to God regularly" (Acts 10:2).

God noticed. An angel appeared to Cornelius:

> "Your prayers and gifts to the poor have come up as a memorial offering before God" (Acts 10:4).

Cornelius's generosity wasn't random charity. It was consistent, openhanded response to God's voice about the needy. God honored it by directing Peter to bring the gospel to his entire household. Cornelius's obedience in generosity positioned him to receive something far greater than he could have orchestrated.

A Modern Boaz Story

Michael owned a small hardware store in rural Kansas—population 3,200. His store had served the community for twenty-two years, generating about $180,000 annually. Enough to employ four people and support his family, but nothing extravagant.

May 2019 brought devastation. An EF4 tornado tore through the county, destroying forty percent of the town. Homes were leveled. Families lost everything. Michael's store sustained damage but remained operational—his building needed about $47,000 in repairs, covered by insurance.

During the chaos of those first days, Michael's accountant called with practical advice: "Use the insurance money to rebuild and modernize. You've been talking about updates for years. This is your opportunity."

It made perfect sense. The store needed better inventory systems, updated point-of-sale equipment, roof repairs that had been deferred. The insurance check would cover it all.

But during his morning prayer two days after the tornado, Michael couldn't shake a thought: "Give away emergency supplies to disaster victims."

He wrestled with it. "God, I need this money. My store needs these repairs. I can't just give away inventory when I have legitimate needs."

The thought persisted. "Be openhanded toward your neighbor who is poor and needy in your land."

Michael recognized the voice. He'd been reading Deuteronomy during his quiet times for months. The command about generosity caught his attention weeks before the tornado—he just hadn't known why it felt so urgent until now.

He made a decision that contradicted his accountant's advice and his own calculations. "I'll give first. I'll trust God for my repairs."

For two weeks, Michael's Hardware became a distribution center. Free tarps for damaged roofs. Free nails, plywood, and basic tools. Free work gloves and safety equipment. No strings attached. No publicity sought. Just openhanded provision for neighbors whose homes had been destroyed.

He served more than two hundred families. His inventory depleted. His insurance money went toward replacing the stock he'd given away instead of modernizing his store.

His accountant thought he'd lost his mind.

But something happened that Michael didn't plan. Local news covered the story—not because Michael sought attention, but because grateful families kept talking about the hardware store owner who gave freely when everyone else was calculating profit margins on disaster recovery.

Regional home improvement chains heard about it. Three different companies approached Michael about partnership opportunities. FEMA disaster relief contracts were directed to his store because of his established reputation for serving the community.

Within eighteen months, Michael's annual revenue increased from $180,000 to $1.2 million.

But that's not the legacy part.

The Ripple Effect Nobody Calculated

Five families Michael helped during those two weeks became volunteers at his store, helping other families navigate insurance claims and rebuild planning. They didn't forget what Michael's generosity meant to them, and they wanted to pay it forward.

Those five families started a community rebuilding nonprofit. Not affiliated with Michael's store. Not sponsored by his business. Just neighbors who'd experienced openhanded generosity and wanted to multiply it.

That nonprofit has rebuilt eighty homes in five years. Families who lost everything now have solid foundations again—literally and financially. The organization employs local contractors, trains young people in construction trades, and creates ongoing economic impact in the community.

Two of the teenagers whose families Michael helped during the tornado, inspired by his generosity and the subsequent community transformation, chose careers in social work and nonprofit management. They're now in their mid-twenties, working in disaster relief organizations in other states, multiplying the ripple effect even further.

Michael didn't plan any of this. He just heard God's voice through Scripture about being openhanded toward neighbors in need, and he obeyed despite the cost.

Ten years later, Michael's store generates consistent profit. His building is modernized. His business is stable. But when you ask him about success, he doesn't point to revenue numbers.

He points to the rebuilt neighborhood visible from his store windows. He points to the nonprofit's office three blocks away, where volunteers coordinate rebuilding projects. He points to the young people who found purpose through serving others.

"Boaz left grain for one widow," Michael says. "That decision put him in the lineage of Christ. I gave away hardware supplies during a disaster. God used it to create a culture of generosity that's still multiplying through our whole town. That's legacy."

Generational Multiplication

Boaz couldn't have known his generosity to one foreign widow would position him in God's eternal redemptive plan. He just heard God's command and obeyed abundantly.

The Good Samaritan didn't know the wounded man's story would become Jesus' primary teaching on neighbor love for two thousand years. He just saw someone in need and responded with openhanded care.

Cornelius didn't know his consistent generosity would position him to receive the gospel and open the door for Gentiles to enter God's family. He just gave regularly to those in need while praying.

Michael didn't know his two-week distribution of hardware supplies would inspire a nonprofit that would rebuild eighty homes. He just heard God say "give" and obeyed despite what it cost him.

God handled the multiplication. God created the ripple effects. God built the legacy.

Your role is hearing His voice and responding in obedience. His role is multiplying it into impact that blesses people you'll never meet in ways you can't calculate.

Questions for Your Heart

1. Who is God prompting you to leave "gleanings" for in your business, work, or daily life?
2. What would happen if you obeyed His voice about generous practices even when it costs you profit or comfort?
3. Whose household could be blessed through your obedience to what you've heard Him say?
4. What legacy is He calling you to build through

listening and obeying His voice about specific neighbors in need?

Prayer

God, show me who You want me to bless through the overflow You've created in my life. Help me hear Your voice directing my generosity toward specific people and families. Give me Boaz's heart—openhanded, abundant, obedient. Give me the Good Samaritan's eyes—seeing need and responding without calculating cost. Give me Cornelius's consistency—regular generosity that honors You. Make my small acts of obedience today blessing that multiplies through generations I'll never see. Let my legacy be written in the lives You direct me to serve. In Jesus' name, Amen.

Key Takeaway

When you hear God's voice directing you toward neighbors in need and respond with openhanded abundance—going beyond minimum obligation to generous provision—He multiplies your obedience into legacy that blesses generations you'll never meet, just as Boaz's gleanings positioned him in the Messiah's lineage and Michael's hardware supplies sparked a community-wide culture of generosity.

Chapter 20

Pure Religion

Hearing God's Voice for Orphans

> "Religion that God our Father accepts as pure and faultless is this: to look after orphans and widows in their distress and to keep oneself from being polluted by the world." (James 1:27)

The verse captured my attention during morning prayer twelve years ago. For weeks, it wouldn't leave me alone—following me through quiet times, surfacing during unrelated sermons, interrupting my thoughts at work.

Look after orphans.

God's Heart for the Fatherless

God's concern for orphans reveals His character. He calls Himself

"a father to the fatherless" (Ps. 68:5).

He

> "defends the cause of the fatherless and the widow" (Deut. 10:18).

Throughout Scripture, He commands His people to care for those without parents.

This isn't optional charity. This is God revealing what matters to Him.

The Crisis and the Response

Millions of children worldwide are orphans—one becomes an orphan every fifteen seconds. Studies show that many become victims of sex trafficking.

The statistics are staggering: hundreds of thousands of children exploited annually in the United States alone. Millions worldwide. Children as young as twelve forced into commercial sexual exploitation.

But statistics weren't what broke our hearts. "These are real people whose childhood has been stolen. If we do not stand up for these children," my wife said quietly, "who will?"

When God Speaks Through Your Church Community

In 2011, our pastor David watched Luke Dowler's music video "Our Silence is Shameful," which portrayed a teenage girl's desperate struggle with sex trafficking. The imagery wouldn't leave him alone. He thought of his wife Lisa's powerful song "Where Has Love Gone?" from her album *You Found Me*.

"You need to create a music video for that song," David suggested to her. "To raise awareness about what's happening right here in America."

Lisa, a gifted singer-songwriter, followed that prompting. She wrote and produced the music video, bringing the hidden epidemic of U.S. sex trafficking into stark visual reality. When "Where Has Love Gone?" released in 2012, it went viral—confronting people with the truth that this happens here, in our cities, to children who could be our neighbors' kids.

My wife and I watched that video together and were deeply impacted. God was speaking to both of us about the fatherless—specifically about children trapped in sex trafficking. The reason was deeply personal. Someone very close to us had been trafficked at a young age. We'd watched her years-long journey toward healing—the nightmares, the shame, the slow rebuilding of trust.

If we could help prevent other children from experiencing that horror—how could we not respond?

As the video spread, David and Lisa recognized that awareness wasn't enough. Survivors needed actual sanctuary. Following God's direction, they founded Destiny House Restoration Center—providing long-term care, holistic therapies, mentorship, music therapy, and job preparation for trafficking survivors.

We were there when this vision was just beginning. We'd prayed as David and Lisa sought God's direction. And now we faced the decision: Would we hear God's voice and respond, or watch from a distance?

From Prayer to Partnership

We didn't start with financial giving. We started with partnership and prayer.

In those early months, Destiny House founders, David and Lisa, needed much support to make this vision a reality including advocates, churches, community leaders, intercessors and of course donors. They were creating a sanctuary for survivors when most churches didn't even acknowledge that sex trafficking happened in America.

We committed to pray regularly—for the founders' protection and wisdom, for survivors who would find Destiny House, for provision. We attended annual benefit concerts. We helped with setup. We invited friends. We showed up—not as distant supporters, but as family members participating in something God was birthing through our church community.

Then came the financial piece.

"What amount can we give every month that doesn't require a miracle to maintain?" we asked ourselves.

We settled on an amount that felt small—almost embarrassingly small compared to the magnitude of the need. But it was sustainable. We could commit month after month, year after year, without crisis or heroics.

"What if God cares more about sustained faithfulness than occasional big gestures?" my wife asked.

Destiny House didn't need us to be heroes once. They needed partners who would stand with them month after month as they walked with survivors through years-long healing journeys.

We set up recurring giving. This wasn't about deciding each month whether we felt like giving. This was about hearing

God's voice direct us toward this specific ministry and building that obedience into our family's financial rhythm.

The first gift felt significant—not because of the amount, but because it represented hearing God speak and responding with sustained action.

Twelve Years of Growing Partnership

That was twelve years ago. Every month since, our giving has continued.

But it hasn't stayed the same. As God has blessed our household and created more margin, He's challenged us to increase our giving. Not because Destiny House pressured us —but because we heard His voice prompting us to give more as He provided more.

Some increases came gradually. Other times, God spoke clearly during prayer: "I've increased your capacity—increase your generosity."

This is what "pure religion" looks like in practice: sustained obedience that grows as God expands your capacity. Not giving when it's convenient, but giving because you heard God's voice and built your response into the rhythm of your life.

Every year, we've attended Destiny House's benefit concerts and awareness events. We've watched the ministry grow from a vision birthed in our small church community to an established organization with over a decade of proven impact.

We've heard update after update: Survivors rescued. Women placed in transitional housing. Aftercare programs providing counseling and trauma therapy launched. Women discovering their God-given identity and destiny.

Every story is a celebration. Every rescued survivor represents a life redeemed from unimaginable trauma.

We've met some of these women at the annual events.

These aren't statistics. These are daughters—beloved by God, advocated for by Destiny House, supported in part by families like ours who heard God's voice and responded with sustained partnership.

But the impact wasn't just on those survivors. This commitment impacted our family.

Our children grew up attending Destiny House events alongside us. They've heard vision updates. They've watched the "Where Has Love Gone?" video that helped birth the vision. They've prayed with us for specific needs.

And sometimes, prompted by God's voice themselves, they've given from their own money toward Destiny House. We didn't force this on them. We simply lived it in front of them—and they caught the vision naturally.

They're learning that our family stands with ministries from inception—not just when it's popular, but through the long obedience of sustained partnership.

The Doubts That Surface

I'd be dishonest if I didn't acknowledge the doubts that have surfaced over twelve years.

There have been months when I looked at our giving and thought, "How can something so small impact something so large?" The global sex trafficking industry generates billions annually. Our monthly giving feels like drops in an ocean.

But then I remember the multiplication stories from earlier in this book. The boy's lunch that fed five thousand. The widow's oil that filled every vessel. God can do more with our little than we can imagine.

There have been moments of financial pressure in our own household when I've wondered if we could afford to continue. But every time, God has proven faithful. As we've blessed their needs, He's continued providing for ours—through consistent, timely provision that reinforces what we learned in Part II.

And there have been seasons when trafficking news felt overwhelming. In those moments, I've had to remember: God isn't asking me to carry the weight of the global crisis. He's asking me to hear His voice about my specific obedience and respond faithfully.

James 1:27 doesn't command me to solve the orphan crisis. It invites me to "look after orphans"—to participate in God's heart for the fatherless within the sphere of influence He's given me.

That I can do. That we have been doing. For twelve years with Destiny House.

What Sustainable Giving Looks Like

If God is speaking to you about orphan ministry—specifically about children vulnerable to trafficking—here's what sustained obedience might look like:

Start with prayer and listening. Don't rush into giving based on emotional response. Ask God to direct you toward a specific ministry or need. Listen for His specific direction.

Consider partnering from inception. We were there when Destiny House was just a vision. Being part of something from the beginning creates deep investment—you're standing with people through the hard work of building.

Determine what's sustainable, not heroic. Better to give $50 monthly for twelve years than $600 once. God values faithfulness over flash. Start where you are. Let God increase it as He increases your capacity.

Make it recurring and consistent. Set up automatic giving. Remove the decision fatigue. When giving becomes rhythm rather than monthly decision, you build obedience into your family's DNA. Ministries can plan around reliable partners.

Participate beyond finances. Attend events. Pray regularly. Show up. Staying connected to the mission keeps your heart engaged and reminds you why you give.

Include your family in the journey. Share age-appropriate information with your children. Take them to awareness events. Pray together for survivors. You're showing them how to hear God's voice and respond across a lifetime.

Trust God's faithfulness to your house. As you bless others from your overflow, God continues providing for your needs. When you participate in His heart for the vulnerable, He demonstrates His heart for your household.

Respond when God challenges you to increase. Don't stay stuck at your initial commitment. As God blesses your work and expands your margin, be ready to hear His voice prompting you to give more.

When God Speaks About Creating Solutions

Some hear God directing them toward sustained monthly giving. Others hear Him calling them to create solutions that address root causes of suffering.

Sam and Linda heard God speak about the orphan crisis in a way that would revolutionize how they approached caring for vulnerable children.

The Hidden Crisis

In 1997, Sam and Linda were supporting an orphanage in Romania. The orphanage directors shared devastating news: thirty to forty children died annually from chronic infections. The children were receiving food, but they were dying anyway.

Sam and Linda learned that over 7 million children worldwide die each year from preventable diseases—not because they lack food, but because malnutrition has compromised their immune systems. When a child's immune system fails, a common cold becomes pneumonia. A bacterial infection becomes deadly.

Sam had worked in the natural supplement industry with immune-optimizing compounds. Research has identified unique molecules that could powerfully support the human immune system.

"What if this could help these children?" They prayed together. Both felt God directing them clearly: *Give it to the orphanage.*

The First Results

They donated a one-year supply of advanced immune support to the Romanian orphanage in 1997.

A year later: The overall health of the children had dramatically improved. For the first time in over a decade, not one child died that year in their organization.

Not one.

Children who had been constantly sick now had energy. Colds didn't turn into pneumonia. Infections that would have been life-threatening resolved.

Sam and Linda sat with that report, tears streaming. "God gave us something that actually works."

Other orphanages heard about the results. Directors began calling. The requests multiplied faster than they could respond individually.

They faced a decision: Was this a one-time gift, or was God calling them to something more?

Founding MannaRelief (1999)

In 1999, they founded MannaRelief Ministries—dedicated to providing immune-optimizing nutritional support to the world's most vulnerable children. The mission: Address the hidden crisis of immune deficiency that kills 7 million children annually despite food aid programs.

MannaRelief started with that one orphanage in Romania. Within years, they were serving orphanages across multiple countries. By 2010, they had provided over 25 million servings of advanced immune support to children in 83 countries.

But they learned something important: The traditional nonprofit model had limitations. Donations fluctuated with economic conditions. Fundraising required constant effort. When the economy struggled, donations decreased—but the children's needs didn't.

They needed a more sustainable solution.

The Social Business Solution

After praying about sustainability, Sam "coincidentally" ran into the original scientist behind the immune-supporting supplement, who shared breakthrough news. He had developed a new extraction process that significantly increased the potency of immune-supporting molecules. He decided to donate the exclusive rights to MannaRelief. "For the children," he and his wife agreed.

Sam and Linda recognized this as God's provision of something revolutionary. That's when they began exploring social business models—companies structured to generate both profit and social impact.

The vision: Create a company that sells advanced health products to consumers. Build a "Buy 1, Nourish 2" model where every product sold provides equivalent support to vulnerable children through MannaRelief.

They launched a social business as a Public Benefit Corporation. Consumers receive advanced health-supporting products. With every purchase, vulnerable children receive immune support through MannaRelief. The business itself becomes the funding mechanism for the mission.

It's a completely different approach than traditional charity, but it addresses the same crisis: children dying from immune deficiency-related diseases.

Twenty-Five Years of Impact

From that first Romanian orphanage in 1997 to today, MannaRelief has provided over 250 million servings of advanced immune support to children in need globally. They now support over 100 orphanages in Mexico alone, plus organizations in over 90 countries worldwide.

Thousands of children who would have died from preventable diseases are alive because their immune systems received the support they needed.

The model evolved from pure charity to include social business—but the mission remained constant: Look after orphans by addressing the immune deficiency crisis that kills them even when they're receiving food.

Two Models, One Heart

MannaRelief still operates as a traditional nonprofit. Donors who prefer monthly giving continue supporting orphanage partnerships through tax-deductible contributions.

But the social business model now provides sustainable funding that doesn't depend on economic conditions or donor fatigue. Customers buying products for their own health simultaneously fund immune support for vulnerable children.

Both models honor God. Both serve orphans. Both demonstrate "pure religion."

My wife and I have participated in both models. For twelve years, we've given monthly to Destiny House Restoration Center, standing with them as they serve trafficking survivors. We've also participated in MannaRelief's social business model, providing thousands of daily servings of life-giving nourishment to vulnerable children around the world.

Both are expressions of "pure religion"—sustained obedience to God's voice directing us toward the fatherless.

The question isn't which model is right. The question is: What is God saying to YOU specifically?

What This Means for You

The global orphan crisis won't be solved by one family's monthly giving or one organization's business model. But God isn't calling you to solve the crisis—He's calling you to hear His voice about your specific obedience.

Some are called to sustained partnership through recurring donations—like my twelve-year commitment to Destiny House Restoration Center.

Others are called to create solutions that address root causes—like Sam and Linda's response to the immune deficiency crisis killing orphans even when they had food.

Others are called to support existing solutions like MannaRelief that combine traditional charity with sustainable business models.

All three approaches honor God. All three serve orphans. All three demonstrate "pure religion."

Is He speaking to you about orphans? About children vulnerable to trafficking? About supporting ministries that provide long-term restoration?

Maybe He's calling you to sustained monthly giving—not heroic amounts, but faithful partnership that continues year after year with organizations like Destiny House.

Or maybe He's birthing something new in your heart—a solution to a problem you've witnessed. An idea that addresses a root cause. Something that seems impossible until you realize it's God speaking.

Maybe He's directing you toward an established ministry already doing effective work like MannaRelief.

If God is speaking, the question isn't whether you have enough. The question is whether you'll hear His voice and respond.

The Progression God Designed

You've learned to worship God with your finances (Heaven). You've learned to trust His provision for your household (House). Now you're learning what it means to love your neighbor—specifically, the neighbor who has no father to advocate for them.

This is the progression God designed: Heaven → House → Nations.

Your house is filled. Your needs are met. Now the fatherless wait. Vulnerable children need advocates. Trafficking survivors need long-term care. Children with compromised immune systems need support that traditional food aid doesn't provide.

Ministries like Destiny House and MannaRelief need sustained support from families who hear God's voice and respond with ongoing commitment—families who will stand with them through years of faithful work.

Some will respond through monthly giving. Others through creating solutions that address root causes. Others through supporting social businesses that fund the mission sustainably.

Will you be one of those people?

Not someday when you have more. Today, with what you have.

Not once, dramatically. Monthly, faithfully. Or through participating in solutions that keep giving.

Not to solve the crisis. To participate in God's heart for those He loves.

James 1:27 defines pure religion. It's simple. It's clear. It's measurable.

Look after orphans.

God is speaking. You're listening. The question is: Will you respond?

The rhythm continues: Heaven → House → Nations.

Your house is filled. Your overflow exists. The fatherless wait for those who hear God's voice about what He calls "pure and faultless."

Questions for Your Heart

1. Is God speaking to you specifically about caring for orphans and the fatherless? What is He saying?
2. What sustainable (not heroic) level of recurring giving could you commit to for orphan ministry or anti-trafficking work?
3. Is God showing you a problem that needs a solution—something you could create or build that addresses a root cause?
4. What would change in your family's culture if supporting orphans became part of your identity, not just occasional charity?

Prayer

Father, thank You for adopting us into Your family when we were orphans spiritually. Thank You for never leaving us or forsaking us. Thank You for providing for our household faithfully.

Now open our ears to hear Your voice about the fatherless. Show us our specific obedience—whether sustained giving to ministries like Destiny House, supporting existing solutions like MannaRelief, or creating new approaches that address root causes of suffering. Give us courage to respond when You speak, even when it costs us comfort or requires risk.

Make us families and individuals who stand with orphan ministry from inception—who pray, who give, who build, who participate in what You call "pure and faultless." Let our obedience to Your voice create impact beyond what we can calculate.

For the sake of children who have no father to advocate for them. In Jesus' name, Amen.

Key Takeaway

Pure religion isn't about which model you choose—monthly giving to ministries like Destiny House, supporting organizations like MannaRelief, or creating new solutions—it's about hearing God's voice directing you toward the fatherless and responding with sustained obedience. Your overflow, whether through donations or participation in innovations that address root causes, becomes God's answer to orphans' prayers when you're listening and He directs you toward them.

Chapter 21

The Vineyard Victory

The vineyard owner departed, leaving his property in servant hands. One servant buried their resources in fear. Some servants doubled his master's investment through faithful stewardship. When the master returned, supernatural rewards followed supernatural faithfulness.

> "Well done, good and faithful servant! You have been faithful with a few things; I will put you in charge of many things. Come and share your master's happiness!" (Matt. 25:21).

Faithful stewardship during the master's absence created eternal partnership in the master's abundance. The servant didn't just get a bonus—he received promotion into joy, responsibility, and intimacy with the master himself.

The faithful servants didn't preserve the master's money—they multiplied it. Fear-based servants bury their gifts to avoid losing them. Faith-filled servants multiply them, understanding that the master judges faithfulness, not just results.

The Shrewd Manager: Using Resources for Eternal Impact

Jesus told another parable about stewardship that reveals how to use earthly resources for eternal purposes.

A rich man's manager was accused of wasting his possessions. The master called him in:

> "Give an account of your management, because you cannot be manager any longer" (Luke 16:2).

The manager faced crisis. About to lose his position, he acted quickly. He called in his master's debtors one by one and reduced their debts—cutting bills in half, forgiving portions of what was owed.

Why?

> "So that, when I lose my job here, people will welcome me into their houses" (Luke 16:4).

The master commended the dishonest manager because he had acted shrewdly.

> "For the people of this world are more shrewd in dealing with their own kind than are the people of the light" (Luke 16:8).

Then Jesus delivered the punch line:

> "I tell you, use worldly wealth to gain friends for

> yourselves, so that when it is gone, you will be welcomed into eternal dwellings" (Luke 16:9).

The manager understood something crucial: earthly resources are temporary tools for creating eternal relationships. Use what you have now—money, influence, property, position—to bless others in ways that matter forever.

Don't just preserve resources. Don't just multiply them for yourself. Use them to create eternal impact in people's lives.

The Requirement and the Reward

Paul stated the stewardship requirement plainly:

> "Now it is required that those who have been given a trust must prove faithful" (1 Cor. 4:2).

Faithfulness isn't optional. It's required. God entrusts resources to you expecting faithful management that multiplies impact beyond personal benefit.

But He doesn't demand faithfulness without offering reward:

> "Whatever you do, work at it with all your heart, as working for the Lord, not for human masters, since you know that you will receive an inheritance from the Lord as a reward" (Col. 3:23-24).

Your stewardship today determines your inheritance tomorrow.

Faithful management of earthly resources positions you for eternal rewards that exceed any temporal return.

Sandra's Downtown Investment

Sandra inherited $50,000 from her aunt—enough to invest safely and secure her financial future. Her financial advisor recommended index funds: 6-8% annual returns, zero risk, steady growth.

But Sandra couldn't stop thinking about downtown. She drove through it daily on her way to her job as a high school English teacher—boarded storefronts, homeless encampments, businesses fleeing to the suburbs. The city had essentially given up.

During morning prayer, a thought kept surfacing: *Invest here. Steward this for your community.*

Her financial advisor thought she was crazy: "Downtown property is the worst possible investment. You'll lose everything."

Her brother agreed: "Aunt Margaret wanted you financially secure. Don't throw her gift away on some idealistic fantasy."

But Sandra couldn't shake the prompting. *Steward this for your community. Invest where others won't.*

Sandra purchased three abandoned storefronts on Main Street for $28,000, borrowed another $30,000 for renovations, and spent the summer updating them—new windows, fresh paint, working plumbing. Simple but hopeful.

By August, she had three spaces ready to rent at $650 monthly—significantly below market rate.

Nine applications came in. Her financial advisor urged her to take the highest-paying tenants. But Sandra had a different standard for stewardship.

She chose three local entrepreneurs who needed opportunity:

Margaret: Running a used bookstore from her garage, passionate about literacy, barely surviving. She could afford $600 monthly—maybe.

James: Army veteran with PTSD, learning to roast coffee as therapy, dreaming of opening a roastery. Disability income was tight.

The Martinez family: Recent immigrants with a food truck, wanting permanent space. Three kids, limited English, enormous work ethic.

Sandra could have rented to established businesses offering $800-900 monthly—safer financially, less risk. Instead, she chose people who needed a chance.

Her financial advisor calculated she'd lose $225 monthly compared to market-rate tenants. "You're a terrible business person," he said.

Sandra smiled. "Maybe. But I'm trying to be a faithful steward."

Year One: Losses on Paper

Sandra's first year was financially brutal.

Margaret's bookstore struggled—some months she could only pay $500. Sandra gave her grace.

James's roaster broke—he missed two months of rent completely. Sandra worked out a payment plan.

The Martinez family faced licensing delays—consistently fifteen days late on rent.

After property taxes, insurance, maintenance, and loan interest, Sandra lost $7,750 her first year.

Her brother sent a sarcastic email: "How's your 'faithful stewardship' going?"

But Sandra noticed something her spreadsheets didn't measure: lights were on in those storefronts. People were gathering. Something was stirring.

Years Two-Three: Community Transformation

Year two, Margaret's bookstore stabilized. She started Saturday morning story time for neighborhood kids. Twenty children showed up the first week. By month six, forty-three kids attended weekly—many from homes with no books.

Margaret expanded the program: after-school tutoring, summer reading challenges, teen book clubs. The bookstore became a community literacy center.

James's coffee roastery found its footing. He hired his first employee—another veteran with PTSD. Then a second. By year three, six veterans worked at his shop. James's roastery became more than a business—it became a safe space where veterans gathered, talked, healed.

Two veterans later credited James's community with saving them from suicide.

The Martinez family's restaurant thrived. They hired three employees from their immigrant community—people struggling to find work because of language barriers. Within two years, the Martinez family helped fourteen immigrant families start their own businesses. Their restaurant became an economic engine.

Year three, other property owners noticed downtown's transformation. Four more buildings were purchased and renovated. New businesses opened. The homeless encampment received city services. A community garden started.

Sandra's three properties now generated $28,800 annually in rent. Her investment worth $80,000 could sell for significant profit.

But Sandra had no intention of selling.

"These properties aren't investments to cash out," she explained. "They're community infrastructure I'm stewarding. My return isn't measured in dollars—it's measured in lives changed, jobs created, hope restored."

Her financial advisor admitted: "I was wrong. You weren't a terrible business person. You were a faithful steward who understood returns I couldn't calculate."

Generational Impact

Ten years later, the ripple effects continue multiplying:

Margaret's literacy program served 197 children. Ninety-seven learned to read at grade level or above. Three became teachers themselves, inspired by the bookstore that changed their lives.

James's roastery employed eighteen veterans total over the decade. Eight started their own businesses. The healing community he created inspired two other veteran-owned businesses downtown.

The Martinez family helped forty-six immigrant families start businesses or find employment. Fourteen of those families now own their own restaurants, employing others from their communities.

Sandra's three storefronts became the catalyst for downtown's complete revitalization. Twenty-three new businesses opened. Property values increased 340%. The city invested in infrastructure. A community that was dying came back to life.

Sandra still teaches high school English. She still drives through downtown every day. But now she drives past thriving businesses, families gathering, children playing in the community garden her investment helped create.

"I stewarded $50,000 for my community instead of my retirement account," Sandra reflects. "Financial advisors said I was foolish. But forty-six families found employment. Ninety-seven children learned to read. Eight veterans found healing. Fourteen families started businesses. A community came back to life."

"That's faithful stewardship. That's eternal reward."

Your Stewardship Opportunity

You have resources God has entrusted to your management. The question isn't whether you have much or little. The question is: Are you faithfully stewarding what you have for Kingdom multiplication?

Will you bury resources in fear or multiply them through faith? Will you steward for personal security or community blessing? Will you measure success by earthly returns or eternal impact?

Questions for Your Heart

1. What resources has God entrusted to your stewardship that you might be burying out of fear rather than multiplying through faith?
2. How would your stewardship change if you measured success by community blessing rather than personal returns?
3. Where is God calling you to steward resources for others' benefit even when it doesn't make financial sense?
4. What eternal rewards await your faithful stewardship that outweigh temporary financial security?

Prayer

Father, help me steward every resource You've entrusted to me with supernatural faithfulness. Give me courage to multiply rather than preserve, to invest for community blessing rather than personal security.

Show me opportunities to steward resources for others' benefit even when it doesn't maximize profit. Help me measure success by Kingdom impact rather than investment returns.

Qualify me for eternal rewards through proven faithfulness in managing earthly resources. Let my stewardship bless my community systematically, not just my household individually.

When I'm tempted to bury resources in fear, remind me that You judge faithfulness, not safety. When faithful stewardship produces temporary losses, give me endurance to continue trusting Your long-term multiplication.

Position me through faithful stewardship for eternal significance that exceeds temporary comfort. Let me hear: "Well done, good and faithful servant. Come and share your master's happiness."

In Jesus' name, Amen.

Key Takeaway

Faithful stewardship measures success by community blessing and eternal impact rather than personal returns—when you multiply resources for Kingdom purposes instead of burying them in fear, stewarding for others' benefit even when it costs you profit, you position yourself for eternal rewards that far exceed temporal comfort, hearing the Master say "well done" for faithfulness that transformed your community.

Part III Summary

Nations Blessed

You came to Part Three with provision for *your* house and a lingering question: **What now?**
You leave with the answer: *your* overflow is often God's answer to someone else's prayer.

What You Discovered About Nations

Through these chapters, you discovered that the journey does not end when *your* needs are met. God filled *your* house so that He could bless *their* house.

The widow's oil that paid her debts continued to flow for others.
A boy's small lunch fed thousands he would never meet.
A net broke with abundance Peter could not contain.
Boaz's generosity blessed generations beyond what he could see.
The widow of Zarephath was sustained through famine by overflow.
A faithful steward heard *"well done"* for managing resources that strengthened his community.
Pure religion revealed itself through caring for the vulnerable in their distress.

You learned to hear God's voice directing you toward specific people with specific needs—and you discovered that obedience creates impact far beyond what you could ever orchestrate.

Nicole's simple obedience of $180 did more than cover one month of childcare for Gloria. It kept her employed, led to a promotion, and empowered her to bless another struggling mother—creating a ripple of provision throughout an entire community.

Your overflow became God's answer to *their* crisis.

Your obedience produced impact in places you may never see, for people you may never meet, through generations you may never live to witness.

The Progression Complete

Heaven positioned your heart to hear God's voice through worship.
House filled your hands as you trusted His provision for your needs.
Nations multiplied your obedience into blessing for others—creating legacy, feeding multitudes, strengthening communities, and building eternal reward.

This is the generous life God designed:

Your overflow becoming His answer to *their* need.

From *your* house to *their* breakthrough.
For His glory.
Forever.

The generous life continues.

Epilogue

Your Money, God's Voice, Your Generous Life

The Question That Started Everything

Years ago, I lay awake at 3 AM asking the question that brought you to this book: "If God owns everything, why does He keep asking for mine?"

The offering plate at church felt like a demand I couldn't afford to meet. Bills were due. My paycheck was stretched. My wife and I had two sons to provide for, and the math simply didn't work.

For years, I wrestled with guilt, confusion, and secret resentment. I loved God. I believed His Word. But His instructions about money felt like one more burden on an already strained budget.

Then I discovered something that revolutionized my entire relationship with finances.

The Discovery That Changed Everything

God doesn't want your money because He needs it. The Creator of the universe isn't experiencing a budget shortfall.

He wants to speak to you about your money because He wants your heart positioned to hear His voice clearly.

> "For where your treasure is, there your heart will be also" (Matt. 6:21).

The voice you follow with your wallet reveals which voice you truly trust with your life.

The Journey Through Impossible Math

My wife and I found ourselves in desperate circumstances. We literally did not have enough to live on, much less consider tithing. The math was brutal and unavoidable.

But we reached a turning point: *What do we have to lose? We don't have enough anyway.*

We stepped out in faith. And everything changed.

Not immediately. Not magically. But steadily, as we learned to hear God's voice about finances and respond in obedience, we discovered that His provision defies human calculation. Our source wasn't our jobs or our skills—it was God Himself.

Once we learned to trust Him with our finances (Heaven), trust His provision for our household (House), we could hear Him directing us to bless others (Nations). We supported ministries caring for orphans and trafficking survivors. We gave beyond what made mathematical sense. And each step confirmed that God's promises are reliable.

What You've Discovered

You've completed the same journey through this book.

Heaven taught you to recognize God's voice calling you to worship Him with your finances. You learned to distinguish His voice from fear's whisper and respond with willing devotion rather than reluctant obligation.

House taught you to trust God's promises about provision for YOUR household. You discovered that His faithfulness to YOUR needs may defy YOUR math, but it proves His Word reliable even when circumstances scream otherwise.

Nations taught you to hear God directing you toward others. You learned that YOUR overflow becomes His answer to someone else's prayer—and that obedience creates impact beyond what you can see or calculate.

Heaven → House → Nations. The progression Jesus established, applied to your finances.

Your Choice Now

You can continue managing your finances according to the world's economics—where the math must always add up, where you can only give what you can afford, where scarcity is your constant companion.

Or you can step into kingdom economics—where God's provision defies spreadsheets, where obedience positions you for breakthrough, and where giving what you don't have opens the door to receiving what you couldn't earn.

The widow with her jar of oil didn't have enough. But when she obeyed the prophet's instructions, God multiplied what she had until her debts were paid and she had overflow.

Abraham didn't have a logical plan when he surrendered Isaac. But his willingness to trust God with his most precious treasure revealed where his true allegiance lay.

The Macedonian churches gave joyfully from deep poverty. The early church practiced radical generosity. The boy's lunch fed thousands. God's mathematics have always defied human calculation.

The Voice You'll Follow

So let me ask you the question one final time:

If God owns everything, why does He keep asking for yours?

You now know the answer: He's not asking for your money. He's asking for your heart.

He's inviting you to hear His voice about your finances and respond with obedient action. To love Him with your wallet. To trust His provision for your household. To bless your neighbor from overflow.

The voice you follow with your wallet reveals which voice you trust with your life.

Which voice will you follow?

And perhaps the most important question still remains...

A Final Invitation

Throughout these pages, one truth has remained constant: God desires relationship, not transaction. That desire is revealed most clearly through **Jesus Christ**, the King who gave Himself so that we might know God, walk in freedom, and live without fear.

If you have never entered into a personal relationship with Jesus—or if your relationship with Him has grown distant—this moment is an invitation. You don't need to have all the answers. You only need a willing heart. Jesus invites you to come as you are and begin walking with Him in trust and faith.

If you sense His invitation, you may respond in your own words, or through the prayer that follows.

A Prayer of Response and Trust

Lord Jesus,

I acknowledge You as the King of my life. I believe that You gave Yourself for me so that I could know God, receive forgiveness, and walk in freedom. Today, I choose to trust You—not only with my eternity, but with my everyday life.

I bring You my fears, my questions, and my concerns, especially in the area of finances and provision. Teach me to hear Your voice clearly and to follow You with faith and peace. I release control, fear, and striving, and I receive Your grace, direction, and rest.

Thank You for loving me, for providing for me, and for inviting me into a life of purpose with You. I choose to listen. I choose to trust. And I choose to follow You.

Amen.

About the Author

Charles D. Harris is a pastor, teacher, and leader with over twenty years of ministry experience, devoted to helping people live purposeful lives aligned with God's plan. He holds a bachelor's degree in engineering from Mississippi State University, but his passion extends beyond professional training to empowering others to discover their God-given potential.

Since 2005, Charles has served as a pastor at One New Man Ministries, where his mission is simple: to *help people win* by guiding them to hear God's voice clearly and respond in faith. His teaching is grounded in real-life experiences and deep biblical principles, shaped by both personal journey and years of pastoral ministry.

Having personally faced the fear and uncertainty of financial instability, Charles understands the struggle of trusting God amid financial pressure. His own journey of faith and breakthrough—especially through learning biblical principles of stewardship, generosity, and the kingdom of God—became a turning point in his life and ministry. Over the years, he has been invited to teach on giving in various churches and ministries, always at the prompting of the Lord and never in pursuit of recognition or compensation. *Why Does God Want*

My Money? is a culmination of the insights and revelations God shared with him during those moments.

Beyond his work in ministry, Charles is a devoted husband, father, and grandfather. He lives in Washington state with his wife, Perry, and enjoys time with their four adult children, daughter-in-love, and five beautiful granddaughters. Raised as the second oldest in a family of eight, Charles learned early to trust in God's provision through every circumstance—a legacy of faith and generosity that continues to shape his life and calling today.

www.ingramcontent.com/pod-product-compliance
Lightning Source LLC
LaVergne TN
LVHW100724061126
851857LV00011B/390